A FIVE @ LEAN ESSENTIALS SERIES

lean essentials for
SCHOOL LEADERS

Shannon R. Flumerfelt, Ph.D.

Charactership Lean Publishing Inc.

TABLE OF CONTENTS

PREFACE

In recent years, school leaders have been challenged with increasingly complex problems to solve. As I have talked with school leaders, I have repeatedly heard administrators self-report that they were 'flat-footed' when leading improvement and managing change. What they were finding was that it was not enough to be sold on an idea for educational reform. What was needed was a toolkit to bring to life the best educational theories for their districts and classrooms. Leaders were responsive and interested in educational best practice, but as they tried to steer both professional and organizational improvement efforts, they were at a loss as to how to actualize the benefits of such. These school leaders were reporting that after repeated attempts to better schools, they were left wondering if the considerable expenditure of time, effort and money, brought forth real substantial, sustainable and scalable accomplishment.

Based on my background in educational restructuring and leadership development over thirty five years, this frustration expressed by school leaders was firmly aligned with my experiences as a school administrator and as a scholar as well. The educational sector is rife with good ideas and has a solid body of knowledge about what is needed to improve schools. Yet, plaguing shortfalls between concepts and reality flourish. The gap between theory and practice is real. I came to believe that the problem of reconciling theory and practice might be best solved with a leadership toolkit, a system of ideas and methods that can be contextualized with some variety for different settings. By working concurrently with both theory and practice by aligned concepts and tools in "pairs," administrators have the flexibility to customize solutions succinctly.

This is when I began to translate a body of knowledge and practice known as lean from other sectors to the educational sector. I approached this work as research and awareness, trying to figure out if lean could work in schools. I found that, in fact, the tools of lean, if implemented in tandem with the tenets of lean, were helpful to school leaders seeking continuous improvement success. That is why I have developed the technology of Lean Essentials, interchangeable tool and concept pairs.

As a caveat, I do not mean to infer that lean is prescriptive. It is not. In fact, lean is extremely organic, relying on problem identification and solution development to emanate from those who work in particular settings and who are impacted by those problems. In creating Lean Essentials, in fact, school leaders are provided with a means of engaging in continuous improvement adaptable to their various cultures and climates.

For those school leaders who applied Lean Essentials to their leadership practice, I discovered that they were able to engage in deep, transformational change. For example, there is the superintendent and administrative team who took three years to learn about lean. They were able to use multiple lean tools to drive strategic planning into daily practice, to eliminate weaknesses in reading instructional practice, to streamline hiring processes, and to roll out technology initiatives with instructional significance. There is also the school district that engaged the assistant superintendent of instruction and the district's instructional coaches in lean training and then used the tools to eliminate repetitive instructional delivery mistakes, to maximize and clarify budget decisions, and to improve mathematics instruction for increased student achievement. These are a few of my experiences with Lean Essentials. Five examples of Lean Essentials are described in detail in the book based on common school leadership challenges.

The purpose of this book is not to provide a scholarly discussion of lean or to present lean research. The purpose of this book is to tell some stories of common problems faced by school leaders today and to provide an explanation of how to use Lean Essentials, concept and tool combinations, to address those problems as models for generalized use. What is proposed for school leaders in this

INTRODUCTION

One of the Five @ Lean Essentials Series, this book is designed for school leaders. The purpose of this book is to provide educational administrators with insight into an organizational philosophy called lean by describing how to use five key tools and concepts to lead continuous improvement via Lean Essentials.

If you are an administrator, you may be wondering, what is lean and why is insight into lean important to me in my role? In short, lean is a long standing, carefully developed, and thoroughly tested set of tools and concepts focused on planning, implementing and sustaining continuous improvement. It is time that schools benefit as much as other sectors have from this base of knowledge and practice.

Lean enjoys recognition as the "gold standard" of organizational practice. This has happened over multiple decades of changes that have occurred as a result of the knowledge and practice of the current age, societal demands, and general environmental factors. For instance, the origins of lean go back to the 1950's, where lean was developed for the manufacturing sector during the next three decades as the automotive industry was unpacked and rethought. The origins of lean are rooted even further back to the 1850's, when the industrial revolution refashioned methods of production based on efficiency and product affordability. The origins of lean link to yet another historical step in the 1750's, when craft production focused on close relationships between artisans and customers in the creation of customized pieces. Lean is highly regarded today because it has been able to "cherry pick" the best tools and concepts from these different eras and bundle them into improved practice. Therefore, pervasive collective interests in improvement lead to redesigning, improving and restructuring when needed; focusing on both quality and efficiency; and relishing the place of customers at the highest levels of the organizational structure. Over time, the best knowledge and practice of this improvement work has emerged and evolved and is known as lean. Now, lean is widely accepted because it gets results and is practical for a variety of core technologies in both product and service-based organizations across all sectors, including private and public organizations.

As lean has moved from its initial straightforward uses on the factory floor to highly complex applications of business intelligence management, there is a growing need for a solid understanding of lean in schools. And it is for this reason that educators are encouraged to engage in lean thinking and applications, as a means of continuous systems improvement on all levels.

This book is presented to school leaders willing to consider the best practices of lean for educational implementation. It is designed to equip the emerging lean leader for a journey of continuous school improvement by highlighting five tools and aligning concepts of lean as Lean Essentials.

A helpful combination of tools and concepts are paired together to enhance lean leadership and to avoid the common pitfall of rolling out lean tools or lean concepts in isolation. Lean initiatives are hard to sustain when employees do not understand WHY they are supposed to use the tools of lean. In addition, lean initiatives are hard to sustain when employees do not understand HOW they are supposed to use the concepts of lean. The merging of both tools and concepts, in contrast, enables leaders and their employees to engage more fully in lean implementation, with a context for both essential ideas and congruent essential actions.

In the following chapters, you will find a visual reminder of the inclusion of both tools and concepts as Lean Essentials. This is done to enable the work of administrators in utilizing lean by equally emphasizing concepts and tools-- and to eventually overlap them in deployment. Further, each chapter describes a concept and a tool and provides a scenario demonstrating how an administrator might use them. The intersection of understanding the concept with the application of the tool is where

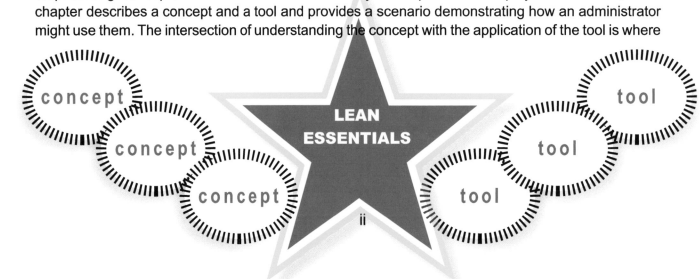

The text also provides several visual cue boxes, highlighted and colored text for clarity in descriptions. Finally, each chapter concludes with a Quick Study section, including Critical Attributes of the Concept, Critical Attributes of the Tool and a Coaching section. The purpose of this last section of the chapter is to provide school leaders with easy-access reminders for lean implementation.

I hope you enjoy the book. But mostly, I hope you enjoy your lean journey!

CHAPTER 1

THE CONCEPT: Eliminate Overproduction
THE TOOL: The Five Why's

THE CONCEPT:
Eliminate Overproduction

LEAN ESSENTIALS

THE TOOL:
The Five Why's

A common technique used in developing lean leaders is to draw a red circle on the floor right in the middle of the busiest activity center in the organization, an office, a hallway, a lunch room, or a classroom, and to ask that manager or leader to stand inside that circle for an hour or more and to observe, to simply watch the work in play. School leaders interested in facilitating lean thinking often start with this type of thoughtful observation in the red circle—noticing the flow and sequence of various processes, trying to understand what is being accomplished that is of value within those processes, and engaging in conversation with those who carry out the work about what can be done to improve those processes. When observation is used and a lean tool called the Five Why's is enacted during learning conversations following the observation, it is possible to collaboratively explore and eliminate a form of waste known as overproduction.

The combination of the lean tool, the Five Why's, and the lean concept, overproduction, is a useful starting point for engaging employees in continuous improvement. This tool and concept provide the dynamics for conversation and deep thinking about process improvement that engages both the leader and the employees in a safe environment. All lean tools and concepts are based on deep respect for people and the desire to improve processes. So it is critical that processes, not people, are observed for improvement and that people are aware and engaged in a culture of observation before proceeding with the Lean Essentials and elimination of overproduction and the Five Why's.

One manager, a lean leader, tells a story about such an observation technique he used in the mail room of a busy office complex. By first establishing a level of comfort with the mail room employees regarding the purpose of and various roles in the pending observation, the manager began. For an hour the manager stood in the red circle, so to speak, and observed the hard working mail clerks drag the heavy bags of mail from the back of the delivery truck to the scales. The clerks knew that the manager was standing in the "red circle" observing them and that this observation would lead to conversations with them about how to bring about mail room improvements, so they worked along through their normal routine. The clerks placed the mail bags on the scales, noted the weight of the bags, and recorded those measures in the appropriate column on a form. With several bags of mail to process each day, this weighing procedure was repeated for each bag of mail. Once the procedure was completed, the mail was then moved to another staging area for sorting and distributing.

After observing the weighing of the mail from the red circle, this manager engaged the two mail clerks in a conversation. The mail clerks and the manager had meet previously and determined that it was important to look for process improvement in the routines and traditions of the mail room. To carry out this conversation, the manager employed a common lean tool, called the Five Why's. The Five Why's is a dialog technique used between two or more people, each with specific roles to fill. One role requires a person to facilitate the "search for the truth" via repeated Socratic questioning and an absence of judgment. The second role requires a respondent or respondents to answer those questions and utilize deeper and deeper levels of critical thinking in order to get to the "real deal." So, the facilitator or manager does not provide the solution for improvement, the respondents or employees figure out the solution as the Five Why's tool is used. This process of Socratic dialogue and critical thinking using the Five Why's is also referred to as root cause analysis in lean.

When the Five Why's are used as a lean improvement tool, it is possible to better understand the value proposition in various processes in two ways. First, the Five Why's will uncover if there is a clear problem statement and shared target condition at hand for a given process. This helps to clarify if the process truly adds value to an operation or if it qualifies as waste. Second, the Five Why's will provide stakeholders, employees, process owners and customers alike, with a shared mental model of a root cause, if one exists. This enhances the chance to optimize the results desired via improving the process under examination.

Keeping this in mind and interested in fostering lean thinking, the manager began this conversation with two of the mail clerks using the first why of the Five Why's, Why #1, "If you are ready to move on, let's use the Five Why's to see if we can improve the processes you are working at. So, here is the first question for you,

'Why do you weigh the mail?'"

One clerk shrugged casually while the other spoke up, "Because we have always weighed the mail."
The manager inquired further using Why #2, "Well, why have you always weighed the mail?"

The bold clerk rolled her eyes and said, "So that we can fill out the column on this form that asks for the weight of the mail." The second shy clerk nodded in agreement.

The manager kept at it, trying to find out the root cause of why the mail was weighed, using Why #3, "Why do fill out the column on that form?"

The outgoing clerk let a laugh escape while the other clerk breathed mild exasperation and interjected, "So that we can keep track of the amount of mail that we process."

The manager nodded and continued using Why #4, "Why do you keep track of the amount of mail you process?"

This clerk now gestured with her hands toward the floor above as the other pointed in the same direction, "So that we can tell administration how much mail we process."

And with a final inquiry using Why #5, the manager asked, "And why does administration need to know this amount of mail that you process?"

The clerks looked at each other with confused expressions and said in unison, "We have no idea. This might be a point of process improvement."

And there it was. The reason for weighing the mail was adrift from a shared understanding of a problem and a target condition. It was simply a routine that had been institutionalized and adopted and repeated. Yet this process was not founded on a root cause analysis—a good reason for weighing the mail. The lean manager and the two mail clerks could see that after a two-minute conversation, a procedure that had taken each clerk several hours of effort each week was a waste of time. There was no justifiable root cause for weighing the mail.

Just to be sure this was the case, the lean manager went to administration and was able to confirm this. Upon further investigation, the manager discovered that there was no reason for weighing the mail from the perspective of any organizational stakeholder—the mail room clerks, the administrators, and certainly not from the customers, the recipients of the mail. There was no reason for recording and reporting the weight of the mail. In fact, the daily burden of lifting the mail bags onto the scales, day after day, week after week, month after month, and year after year, added no value to the goal of getting the mail out to its recipients quickly. Beyond that, there was the waste of motion to move the mail bags around in the mail room, on and off the scales, a lot of unneeded wear and tear on the backs of the mail clerks day after day, week after week, month after month and year after year. It was also easy to see that additional waste spilled over into the useless paperwork that was generated from this process. The work of gathering the reports on the weight of mail, forwarding them from the mail room to administration, represented a significant effort in the mail room day after day, week after week, month after month and year after year. And the generation of those reports had no value for administration or carried any weight in decisions made in regard to mail room operations.

This problem of "weighing the mail," is an example of how easy it is to slip into the creation of unnecessary work and to use human capital to engage in that work for no viable reason. For purposes of simplicity and because there are eight forms of waste in lean, let's focus on the most glaring of the eight in this example, the waste of overproduction. This most prominent form of waste in the mail room involved the work of doing more than was required, from weighing the mail bags, filling out the forms and generating the reports. This form of waste is identified in lean as overproduction, a lean key concept.

In fact, this form of waste, overproduction, is one of most common types of waste in schools, too. As school leaders create a culture for observation and continuous improvement, then stand in the red circle and observe a few key processes that take place all around them, and finally create Socratic dialog and critical thinking around the Five Why's, chances are that this form of waste, overproduction, will surface. The Lean Essentials, the Five Why's and eliminating overproduction, are very powerful in school improvement work.

Let's consider, for instance, a small school district with one high school. This district's high school proudly offers an intervention program they created in response to their concern over the increasing high school dropout rate. The program they created involves identifying all high school students who have failed one class in the past three semesters. Once identified, these students were then assigned to a weekly teacher advisor program. Trained teachers and these at risk students met once a week in small groups with other students who have also failed a class. The teacher advisor time was offered to these at risk students only, which meant other students in the school ended their day early once a week.

After using the Lean Essentials, the Five Why's tool and the concept eliminating overproduction, it was uncovered how this intervention program could be better. The intervention program was an example of overproduction, because although well intentioned, it represented an added on process absent root cause analysis. The school had identified the at risk students and knew that they wanted to do something about assisting those students, but they did not use root cause analysis to do so. The teacher advisor program sounded like a good idea at the time to this school, but without engaging in a root cause analysis of the problem of increasing dropouts via the Five Why's, an opportunity for improvement was being missed and overproduction resulted. This intervention program is much like weighing the mail program because it created an additional layer of service without causing improvements to the core process of instructional delivery as an intervention to failure.

After creating a culture of observation and continuous improvement, a new superintendent stood in the red circle of this high school, so to speak, and prepared to use the Lean Essentials, the Five Why's and eliminating overproduction, in a dialog with the high school principal and assistant principal. The high school principal and assistant principal were very interested in driving school improvement and in doing so without wasting resources, so they were eager to engage in this conversation.

The superintendent began the Socratic dialogue with the administrative team using Why #1, "Let's look at the teacher advisor program today. I have observed it and would like to run through the Five Why's with you both. So, let's begin with the first why, why do you offer the teacher advisor program at this high school?"

The assistant principal shrugged casually and the principal responded with a puzzled brow, "Because we need to decrease the dropout rate."

The superintendent inquired further using Why #2, "Well, why did the dropout rate increase?"

The principal rolled her eyes and threw a glance to the assistant principal, "Because more students than ever do not pass their required classes. They get discouraged and then drop out of school."

The superintendent kept at it using Why #3, "Why do more students than ever not pass their required classes?"

The principal breathed mild exasperation as the assistant principal stepped in, "Because they do not like their classes or do not want to do the work required to pass."

The superintendent nodded and continued using Why #4, "Why do these students not like their classes or not want to the work required to pass?"

The principal now gestured with her hands toward the hallways above, "Because they don't like the topics, they don't like the teacher, they don't have the skills or background to understand the material." The assistant principal added confidently, "You see, there are so many reasons why."

And with a final inquiry using Why #5, the superintendent asked, "And why are there so many reasons that students drop out? What you have described to me is an instructional system that requires students to spend time in the teacher advisor program after failing a class. If there are problems in the classroom experience when the student is in class in the first place, then why don't we address those problems when they occur instead of working around them after the problem has occurred?"

The principal and assistant principal turned to each other with confused looks on their faces and stated in

The Five Why's	An organizational tool for root cause analysis
Overproduction	A common form of waste resulting from a lack of root cause analysis

Upon further investigation, the superintendent, principal and assistant principal agreed that the teacher advisor program did have some ancillary benefits for the school. But as a solution to an educational delivery system that allowed a student to sit in class for a whole semester, fail the class due to lack of interest, lack of effort, or lack of skills; and subsequently to get assigned to a teacher advisor on a weekly basis for support was much like weighing the mail. It was a form of overproduction and it further allowed the root cause of the problem to remain firmly in place.

The teacher advisor program is an example of overproduction because required a lot of work on the part of the faculty and students yet failed to address a root cause of student failure via process improvement. The program was well planned and everyone was trying hard to make it work. It did require a substantial investment of district resources in program planning and implementation, teacher training, student/parent orientation, and a weekly one-hour allocation of teacher time. It also required students who were passing classes to give up twenty minutes of instructional time each week. So, the investment of time, effort and resources was substantial for the entire school community. However, the allocation of resources to a program, even as the program was carefully administered, was a form of overproduction because the program did not solve the root cause of the problem; it worked around it. Furthermore, when overproduction is present, as it was in this program, the repetitive process of running the teacher advisor program week after week, month after month, semester after semester represents ongoing overproduction. When overproduction is present, it requires resources to support it, therefore, the core technology, the delivery of instruction in the daily classroom, is not impacted nor improved via this initiative. The delivery of instruction in the daily classroom was left out of the improvement cycle. Further, it caused a reduction of twenty minutes per week of instructional time. The lack of root cause analysis actually created additional waste and left the constraints in the current educational delivery system firmly in place.

This program is an example of overproduction because the school spent substantial resources, both financial and human, adding an additional program to an existing educational delivery system in lieu of conducting a root cause analysis and improving that system. Therefore, school district was doing more than was required, adding an additional layer of programming, engaging in overproduction.

What is interesting about the condition of overproduction is that this form of waste is especially hard on schools with limited resources. This is because overproduction causes the diversion of funds to new programs and it also sets up the dynamics for avoidance of root causes. So, now as a result of overproduction, the district not only has an additional program to fund and support, but it also still has the same problem it started out with. As overproduction plays out, there will never be enough additional programming to curtail the problem, no matter how hard the school tries because the root cause, shortcomings in the traditional delivery of high school instruction, are not addressed. The irony is that by doing too much by way of overproduction, this teacher advisor program will never be enough.

It is for this reason that overproduction is a particularly painful form of waste. Overproduction is a terrible misuse of the capacity of the organization because it misallocates the talents and contributions of people without producing value. Overproduction actually stabilizes dysfunction to the degree of institutional acceptance of the shortfall. This means that this school did have to do more with less in the worst sense by having to work hard to deploy a program that enabled the root cause to continue to function.

As the superintendent observed this form of overproduction in the high school, he was very concerned that the resources allocated to the teacher advisor program did undermine the capacity of the district. He concluded that not only had resources been used to "work around" an educational delivery system sorely in need of improvement, but that the effort that went into this program prohibited the high school from fully developing the capacity of its instructional program. It was wasting the talents and contributions of the teachers when they were sorely needed to improve classroom instruction.

By using the Lean Essentials, the lean tool the Five Why's and the lean concept of eliminating overproduction, this superintendent was able to refocus the high school administrators and school improvement team on the school's core operation, classroom instruction. And what these employees found is that the work of improving instruction in a high school is very different from the work of providing a teacher advisor program as a workaround. In fact once the problem of overproduction was identified, it was possible for this high school to tie the intentions of the teacher advisor program directly into the classroom experience when the assistance was needed, not after the student failure had occurred.

The Lean Essentials, eliminate overproduction and the Five Why's, are easy-to-use methods when observation uncovers the potential that value can be created. These Lean Essentials are the basics, not for judging people, but for collective inquiry into gaps where workarounds to problems are occuring and for collective problem solving.

Critical Attributes of the Concept: Eliminate Overproduction

- This concept is a common and hard to see form of waste.
- The concept involves doing more than what stakeholder values, which creates waste.
- This concept is about changing habits that are embedded in routines and traditions to obtain process improvement, not to pick on people.

Critical Attributes of the Tool: The Five Why's

- Use the tool within the context of a culture of observation and as learning conversation for process improvement.
- Use the tool based on Socratic dialog, assigning clear roles and asking why several times.
- Keep asking why to obtain the root cause of the constraint.

Lean Leadership Coaching:

To begin using the Five Why's and eliminating overproduction:

1. Select a functional area that you know needs improvement.
2. Contact the employee responsible for the functional area and indicate that you would like to work together to improve it by conducting an observation (not an evaluation).
3. Go to where the work takes places and conduct an observation considering key metrics, flow, barriers, and routines of work.
4. Identify a single process within the functional area where you have observed waste, overproduction, and engage the employee in a discussion of the Five Why's.
5. Agree on a root cause of the waste with the employee.
6. Collaboratively solicit ideas for elimination of the waste.
7. Assign someone to work with stakeholders to fix the problem.

CHAPTER 2

THE CONCEPT: Learning to See Waste
THE TOOL: Value Stream Mapping

THE CONCEPT:
*Learning To
See Waste*

LEAN
ESSENTIALS

THE TOOL:
*Value Stream
Mapping*

The tools and concepts of lean help to create clarity around intentions outlined in mission, strategic planning and vision. The Lean Essentials of learning to see waste and value stream mapping enable iterations of shared meaning to develop as lean leaders and employees alike conduct interactions and complete work focused on the creation of value. In this chapter, you will learn how to engage these Lean Essentials.

To begin to understand the Lean Essentials, learning to see waste and value stream mapping, presented in this chapter, recall your organization's mission statement and consider what it means in relation to daily work. Your mission may read something like this:

>   The mission of my district/school
>   is to help all students to --
>   become life-long learners,
>   OR reach their full potential,
>   OR develop skills for the 21st century,
>   OR become productive citizens . . .

Regardless of the exact wording, if your mission statement aligns with any of the above samples, you have clearly identified those you serve. In these examples, students are the stakeholders served; they are the intended beneficiaries of the best educational service your district can provide.

Your organization may have a mission statement that is slightly different from the examples listed above; it may be more like this:

> The mission of my district/school
> is to provide to our COMMUNITY—
> 	-centers of excellence,
> OR -student-centered learning environments,
> OR -personalized learning experiences,
> OR -equal opportunities for all learners. . .

If your mission statement resembles the intentions of these above samples, then it also provides a clear definition of those served. The community is the critical stakeholder, the recipient of the best educational service your district can provide. In contrast, a school leader would not endorse a mission statement such as:

> The mission of my district/school
> is to deliver to BUILDING ADMINISTRATORS—
> 	-the most efficient protocol for scheduling instruction,
> OR -the easiest code of conduct to enforce,
> OR -the highest budget allocation for co-curricular instruction.

While, such a mission statement describes the ancillary benefits of well run building operations, as a focus statement it is offbeat from mission because it identifies building administrators as critical stakeholders served; those benefitting from the district's services. While building administrators are internal stakeholders of the district, they are not the focus of district mission as its essential customers of instructional services. The obvious problem with this last awful sample mission statement is that the critical stakeholders, the students and/or community, are not accounted for. Therefore, such mission statements would not be articulated. Yet, while not intended, desired critical stakeholders may not be recognized in reality if a perspective (or culture) shifts or drifts away from mission. In such cases, as critical stakeholders fade, it is impossible to deliver the value promised in the mission statement.

In fact, when value is not delivered to critical stakeholders, then this means that waste is present. And this is why the Lean Essentials of learning to see waste and value stream mapping are helpful. As critical stakeholders are identified and value is understood from their perspectives, waste also emerges, and mission is emphasized. In fact, in using the Lean Essentials, learning to see waste and value stream mapping, the presence of waste provides an opportunity to improve and create value where it is absent. To understand the relationship of value and waste, let's explore the last offbeat mission statement again by replacing the misplaced critical stakeholder role from administrators to the properly cited critical stakeholder role to students. This will provide contrast between value creation and waste elimination for these roles.

The mission of my district/school is to deliver to **students**-- the most efficient structure for instruction,

VALUE TO BE CREATED:
*(meaning that creating the most efficient structure for **students** may be)*

- to create access to the best teacher lecturers on given topics to expedite time used for lectures to learning gained
- to provide a variety of learning options to increase propensity to learn based on learning preferences
- to allow students to enter and leave learning based on mastery of expectations to decrease "seat time" and increase time used to learn new things
- to use technology to increase just in time student access to teachers to reduce the time gap between inquiry and practice, and
- to create additional time for students to access learning opportunities beyond the classroom for applications-based learning opportunities.

In order to create value for **students** in terms of increasing efficiency in high school instruction given a limited pool of resources, then waste must be eliminated. There are two interrelated ways to create value. The first way is to create value by understanding who the critical stakeholder is and what needs to be done to create value. The second way is to eliminate waste by understanding who the critical stakeholder is not and what does not need to be done to eliminate waste. The creation of value is a trade off to the elimination of waste by shifting the focus to the mission's critical stakeholder and replacing misaligned critical stakeholder roles.

To revisit the formerly presented offbeat mission statement, the waste to be eliminated by replacing the misplaced critical stakeholder role from administrators to the properly cited critical stakeholder role to **students** can also be identified in order for value to be created.

WASTE TO BE ELIMINATED:
*(meaning that replacing the most efficient structure for **administrators** to eliminate waste may be)*

- to not have students attend the same classes every day with the access to the same teachers and
- to not allocate class time in a standardized way for all students.

13

Yet, if one closely examines the daily educational experiences of typical high school students, this least desirable mission statement may be well what these critical stakeholders, **students**, traditionally encounter. In traditional high schools, while not intended, there may be lots of waste occurring in instructional delivery for **students** as the learning experiences is a process that is based on 1) a semester- or year-long repeating schedule that counts seat time as a valued metric with exposure to a limited pool of teachers and 2) standardized allocations of class time offering repetitive blocks of minutes for learning.

While mission statements are typically quite straightforward, they are hard to enact if critical stakeholders are not served by core processes. There may be a challenge before school leaders in enacting the mission statement in a way that delivers results to the critical stakeholders identified. The Lean Essentials, learning to see waste and value stream mapping, are presented to assist school leaders in this work. Your mission statement, if taken seriously, can help to enact the Lean Essentials using the concept of learning to see waste by examining the value proposition for your key stakeholders in educational delivery through value stream mapping.

Let's examine again the typical district mission statement and consider how the delivery of services is experienced by critical stakeholders, **students**. Here are the sample mission statements again:

> The mission of my district/school
> is to help all students to–
>> become life-long learners,
>> OR reach their full potential,
>> OR develop skills for the 21st century,
>> OR become productive citizens . . .

So, if **students** are the critical stakeholders of mission and if what they value is described as becoming life-long learners, or as reaching their full potential, or as developing skills for the 21st century, or as becoming productive citizens, then a walk in the shoes of the **students** to understand if this mission is realized or not is a good place to start to use the Lean Essentials, learning to see waste and value stream mapping. In the following description, look for critical stakeholder value creation and critical stakeholder waste elimination.

In typical traditional high school educational delivery systems, students are placed on standardized plans of study. There is little space within the traditional educational delivery system to consider the level of personal mastery students possess. While content mastery is taught for and tested extensively, there is no structured approach to competency development required for success in the 21st century. Students are moved from class to class based on an assembly line mentality, befitting of a factory where teachers are the workers and students are the products that come to them. Because of a focus on meeting standardized testing requirements, the students have to move quickly through a series of daily lessons or classes, with little time for in depth experiential learning, reflection, and real world application. And while students are expected to fully trust the educational system they attend, they have little reciprocal trust demonstrated toward them to facilitate the development of lifelong learning acumen and self-directness by having the opportunity to make developmentally appropriate learning choices for themselves.

While this description may not represent the learning experiences of high school students in your district, it is important to understand that whatever those educational experiences are, if they are not valued by **students**, those critical stakeholders you serve, then those learning experiences contain waste and are in need of improvement.

The Lean Essentials, learning to see waste and value stream mapping, can help school leaders to drive improvement based on what critical stakeholders value. The tool, value stream mapping is a visual management tool that makes waste easy to see. This tool will be described in detail later. In lean, there are eight forms of waste. Overproduction, previously described in Chapter One, is first on the list:

- Overproduction-Adding extra features or services that are not valued by the critical stakeholder.
  Example: Responding to every demand by trying to do everything for everyone, instead of focusing on what is needed to create value for critical stakeholders so that mission is not lost in daily work.

- Inventory-Providing additional materials or requirements that are not needed to complete the work.
  Example: Adding extra requirements for students to programs to create job security, instead of reducing requirements to meet essential outcomes so that the right amount of service is provided.

- Extra Processing Steps-Creating extra steps, black holes, and dealing with redundancies that do not add value.
  Example: Auditing to the degree that everything is checked, instead of designing mistake-proofing to free up employees so that checking does not consume resources, instead of creating improvement opportunities when mistake proofing fails.

- Motion-Finding or searching for information or resources that are needed, but cannot be found without engaging in movement to get to the source.

Example: Waiting to go to class to obtain information from the teacher, instead of accessing a teacher website or database developed by teachers with course information.

- Defects-Discovering that process problems created shortfalls or defects at the end of the line, wasting resources by creating, accepting or passing along apparent problems.

  Example: Summatively assessing students at the end of the marking period and discovering then that most of the students failed to understand course material, instead of a working with teachers to monitor student progress on a daily or weekly basis and intervening as needed so that marking period assessment creates better results.

- Waiting-Allowing time to lapse because of dysfunction leading to missed deadlines, wasting employee and stakeholder time.

  Example: Retaining an advanced student in a prerequisite course based on board of education policy when the student has mastered the course content, instead of allowing a student to test out of a course and to take a more advanced course.

- Transportation-Handing off people, materials, or resources by relocating them to a different location, wasting time and energy to move then.

  Example: Maintaining central storage of books and supplies by an Operations Manager for the various district facilities which requires a transportation move to get the materials to where they are needed, instead of shipping the materials directly to the point of need to save time, steps and energy costs.

- Knowledge Loss-Permitting the talents, knowledge and wisdom of staff to go unrecognized or to get lost, wasting the social capital of an organization by cultural deficits and communication problems.

  Example: Allowing the expertise of the faculty to remain private, instead of rewarding, celebrating and recognizing that master teachers could mentor new teachers, all faculty could participate in instructional observation and improvement or lead collegial groups to improve both explicit and tacit building knowledge.

The key for any school leader concerned about the quality of learning experiences provided to critical stakeholders, whether they are the students, community, or employees, is to realize that a clear direction for improvement of the organization is in front of all stakeholders every day in the mission statement. This is often difficult to comprehend at first, but by employing the Lean Essentials, the tool of value stream mapping

mapping and the concept of learning to see waste, it is possible to enhance understanding as to what the desired goals in the mission statement have to do with the current reality of the daily operation of the district or school and where waste is taking the district away from mission or other critical goals and plans. The lean tool, value stream mapping, and the lean concept, learning to see waste, provides an explicit way to make connections between a desired future reality and the present. By aligning critical stakeholder needs with the present state, future improvement needs are clear.

The tool of value stream mapping and the concept of learning to see waste can help to bring clarity to your mission statement or other framing documents through a two-step process. The first step is to identify your stakeholder and walk in the shoes of your stakeholder, all the while measuring the quality of the stakeholder's experience against a metric that reflects critical stakeholder value. The second step is to use visual management techniques to create corporate conversations about what is lacking or not working, where waste is occurring and what is in need of improvement.

So, if the critical stakeholders are your students, this means that your students should receive maximum value from your schools. Similar to standing in the red circle and observing processes as described in Chapter One, value stream mapping is an act of leadership that requires you to do something that might seem strange for a school leader. Value stream mapping requires deeply understanding what your critical stakeholders experience in order to take on their perspectives. You want to understand not what you think is valuable, but you want to understand what your stakeholders think is valuable. In order words, value is determined by the critical stakeholder, not by others.

And as a complementary concept to understanding value from the perspective of the critical stakeholder, identification of waste is also up to this constituent—whatever is not valued, is, therefore, considered waste. Value stream mapping is a visual management tool that will help you and your employees to collectively understand where waste is occurring; it will help you to see waste as a corporate problem. The point of the Lean Essentials, value stream mapping and learning to see waste, is for your district to be able to deliver value to your critical stakeholders when they want it without waste.

Learning to see waste is a concept that is most of us encounter regularly. So, once it is comprehended in daily life, it is easier to apply to work. Since the role of being the critical stakeholder is fairly easily to understand as a retail customer, the following example highlights how essential learning to see waste is and what it means to mission and goals.

> *Consider, for example, a critical retail stakeholder, a hotel business traveler. This businessperson is weary from travels and approaches the front desk upon arrival at the hotel. With a forced smile and anxious to get checked in, the customer provides the information requested by the polite desk clerk. Noticing that the information is written by hand instead of being entered into the computer, the customer is not surprised to learn that the "check in system" is down. However, the customer is disappointed to find out that check-ins are delayed for 15 minutes. The only option for the customer is to sit in the lobby until the check in system is repaired.*

> *The customer knows that this is not the usual process for hotel patrons checking in when the computer system is down. Most hotels would immediately revert to a manual check in system in an effort to deliver the best possible experience to the customer. Sitting in the lobby, the customer counts a steady stream of customers facing the same problem, not being able to check in. As the 15 minutes wait expires and turns into two hours, the computer system is still not repaired. During this time, one clerk is manning the front desk while several other employees carry on their normal duties, seemingly oblivious to the growing crowd of patrons waiting for room assignments. No doubt, behind this front desk scene was a lone computer programmer frantically trying to repair the system. As the customers sit in the lobby, conversations take place between them questioning why the hotel does not abandon the notion of using the computerized check in system while it was being repaired and conduct a simple manual check in instead. The patrons see the waste very clearly.*

In the case of this scene in the hotel lobby, the desk clerk and other employees were not walking in the shoes of their customers. In fact, in terms of value stream mapping, it appeared that the hotel's critical customer was not the patron at all, but that the computerized check in system was. This hotel had a value stream map in use, but it did not have its hotel patrons as its critical customers during this computer crisis. It had placed the computerized check in system as the critical customer. This was obvious because the management team made the decision to allocate all resources to fixing the check in system and to carrying out normal duties, rather than to accommodating the hotel patrons.

It may seem odd that the computer system became the customer, while people sat in the lobby. But, this is a fairly common problem in most organizations. In short, the loss of who your critical customer is in any process indicates that vertical coordination is functioning apart from core mission and other essential goals. To understand what this means for schools, let's examine a similar scenario in education where the critical customer differed between a school administrator and a teacher.

> *A new teacher with a first semester of instruction under her belt loves her new job. Every day she stops in the front office to pick up her mail and sees the assistant principal on a daily basis. As the second semester begins, she decides it is important to ask the assistant principal for some informal feedback on her teaching. As she picks up her mail in the front office one morning and notices the assistant principal is standing nearby, she greets the administrator and asks, "Now that I have finished my first semester, I know that there is a formal review process I will go through, but could you give me your informal impressions of how my first semester went." The assistant principal replies, "Sure, the way that I look at it is that if I have no parent complaints, this means that you are doing fine." The new teacher walks away stunned, confused and disenfranchised.*

In terms of value stream mapping, the critical stakeholder is very different for the assistant principal and the new teacher. For the assistant principal, the critical stakeholder is the complaining parent. The assistant principal is ready to spend time and effort if a complaint comes in from a parent and is interested in delivering service to that parent. For the teacher, the critical stakeholder is the student, not the complaining parent. The teacher is spending time and effort delivering the best instruction possible to the student every day. The critical stakeholders are very different for these two employees in the school, and, therefore, the value stream maps they are working off of are also very different. In terms of school mission and school improvement goals, the teacher is clearly working to manage value to the students. The administrator is working to manage value to a different stakeholder, the complaining parent. Value stream mapping can quickly clear up these types of problems and create either a shared critical stakeholder of the process or recognition of critical stakeholders of the enterprise. From that point, it is easier to determine what work is and is not aligned with mission and goals.

This is also where the hotel management team went wrong because there was nothing in the mission statement of the hotel that refers to the check in system as the critical customer. The customers that mattered on that particular day surrounded the management team and sat right in the hotel lobby. What should have happened is that when the computer system broke down. Measures should have been taken so as to create value for critical customers. This would eliminate patrons having to experience any form of waste. Each of these patrons no doubt had plans that were delayed and negatively impacted. Unfortunately, no one in management could see the waste that this critical customer understanding was producing for the patrons in the form of waiting. They were not walking in the shoes of their patrons. If they were, they would have moved to a manual check in system immediately without making the check in system malfunction a problem for the patrons. This solution was obvious to each patron sitting in the lobby as waste is always most obvious to the customer. The best move for management to make would have been to consider what the customer finds most valuable given the broken system by asking them. Unfortunately, the patron was not the critical customer in this incident, so this perspective was not in play.

In the case of the new teacher and school administrator, the critical stakeholders were recognized, but they were different. When the teacher asked for feedback, she was doing so from the shoes of her students. When the administrator provided feedback, she was doing so from the shoes of her parents. In either case whether there is a failure to identify the critical stakeholder or if different critical stakeholders are of concern, this can cause confusion and waste. Failure to execute to mission is often the result of this problem.

Identifying your critical stakeholders and then walking in their shoes can be accomplished with a lean tool called value stream mapping. This tool is used so that the concept of learning to see waste as specified by the stakeholder occurs as a collective act of improvement in the district. When the district's employees have an opportunity to agree on who the stakeholder is and then to see where waste occurs, those areas emerge as shared constraints and become points of improvement. The Lean Essentials, the value stream map and learning to see waste, do just that through collaborative visual management techniques.

Value stream mapping uses common icons. When you begin with identification of the stakeholder and follow with a mapping process from the perspective of that stakeholder, the icons of value stream mapping make this easy to do. The mapping process is broken into process steps and the process steps are examined using a metric, such as time, quality, student attitudes, achievement standing, or cost of labor. When the whole process is mapped out and measured with icons, the value stream map becomes a useful visual management tool that prods discussion about value and waste, value creation and waste elimination, and, ultimately, improvement. As with the scenario where the teacher solicited informal feedback from the assistant principal, it would have been better if the assistant principal would have asked the teacher which stakeholder she wanted feedback from or qualified her feedback by recognizing that parent feedback represents one critical stakeholder group and students represent another.

To begin value stream mapping, the stakeholder is associated with a unique icon, a crooked crown. Identifying the stakeholder may seem like an obvious first step, but in the case of the hotel with the check in system problem, the essential customer was missed or misidentified. In the case of the school with the new teacher and administrator, the stakeholder was not shared. So this is first step may lead to some foundational discussions about the purpose of a process as it relates to mission and goals.

The following example illustrates how the initial stages of value stream mapping can enlighten identification of critical stakeholders. Here is where the value stream mapping incorrectly began for the hotel patron check in process:

Instead, aligning with their mission statement and identifying the patron in the check in process as the customer in value stream mapping should look like this:

For the school with the new teacher and the administrator, here is how the value stream maps differed:

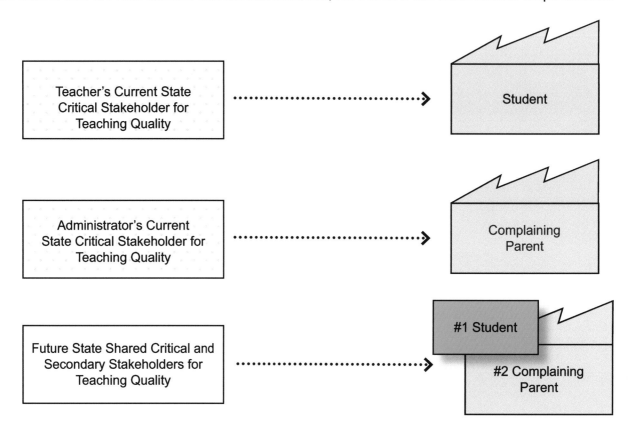

For both the hotel and the school, aligning with their mission statements and identifying shared critical stakeholders in the instructional delivery process, will look like the above diagrams. Once the critical stakeholder is identified (or prioritized), value stream mapping fosters the concept of learning to see waste because two value stream maps are produced.

In the case of this hotel's check in process, the first improvement to be made with a value stream map is to clarify who the customer is. The current state map initially indicated that the check in process when the system is down creates waiting waste for the critical customer. Once improvements are explored to alleviate waste in the current state, then a new future state map places the hotel patron as the critical customer with a check in process that eliminates waste and creates value.

In the case of the school's process for providing quality teaching, the first improvement made based on the current value stream map is to clarify who the critical stakeholders are. In reality, there are two different critical stakeholders and two different current state maps operating in the conversation between the teacher and the administrator. In comparing the two current state maps, the school may determine that the complaining parent serving as the critical stakeholder is poor process design for instructional delivery in the classroom. After discussion about the role of the parent in determining quality of teaching in the school, it may be decided that the complaining parent should be considered on the future state map, but not featured as the critical stakeholder over the student. A new future state map now identifies the student as the shared critical stakeholder for determining quality teaching and recognizes the complaining parent as the secondary stakeholder. This future state value stream map now provides an important role for the parent in the instructional delivery process as a secondary stakeholder, without replacing or diminishing the critical stakeholder, the student.

Under the new future state map, the conversation between the new teacher and the administrator would unfold differently. Clarification regarding the critical or secondary stakeholders assists the teacher and administrator in meaningful dialog. As the teacher asks the administrator for information on the teacher, separate responses to student feedback and parent feedback can be shared. Instead of the teacher feeling confused about the administrator's comments, a shared understanding of how stakeholders are prioritized in regard to teaching quality create a better conversation.

Filling in the critical stakeholder box in the current state value stream map for processes in schools does require some thought as well. It is best to be honest about who that stakeholder actually is so that waste is removed on that basis. If the critical stakeholder box is correct in the current state value stream map, then the next step is to lay out the process as experienced by that stakeholder and to look for waste. By taking the process apart step by step, measuring the impact of each step against a metric, and learning to see waste, it is possible to build improvement into current practices.The taking apart of a process is represented on a current state value stream map. The putting back together of a process is represented in a future state value stream map (known as kaizen in value stream mapping, described in detail in Chapter Four).

Consider, for example, the high school from Chapter One concerned about their high school graduation rate. This concern led them to create a process called the teacher advisor program. In its current form as an intervention after the student fails, we know from root cause analysis and using the Five Why's that this is a process loaded with the waste, overproduction. So, in the current state value stream map of this teacher advisor process, one would hope that this process aligns with the district's mission and retains the student as the critical stakeholder. If the student is the stakeholder, then the current value stream map will identify what is in the stakeholder's value stream and what is waste. Kaizen will provide for the transition from the current process to an improved future process.

In the case of this high school with the teacher advisor program from Chapter One, the critical stakeholder is the student. This is not a problem for this district and high school. However, the rest of the current value stream map will uncover exactly where value and waste occur through process analysis and metrics. After the first current state is created and points of improvement are identified through kaizen work, depicted on a current state map as a kaizen burst, then a future state map is created.

To create the current and future state value stream maps, the customer icon is used, along with several other icons. The critical customer/stakeholder icon has already appeared in this text. For the sake of simplicity, we will use seven basic icons in this chapter to demonstrate the tool of value stream mapping and the concept of learning to see waste:

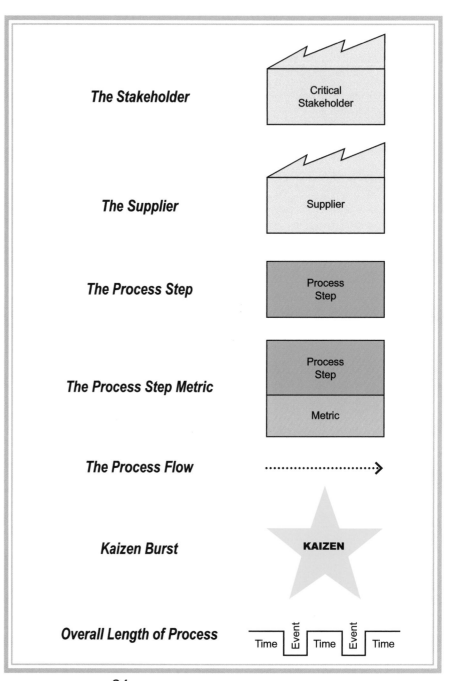

The current state value stream map of the teacher advisor program is created first. On this map the average at-risk student is the stakeholder.

The State Department of Education, teachers, college admissions offices and the Board of Education are suppliers. The relationship among the suppliers is indicated along with a metric of interest. The relationship between the suppliers and the student is indicated along with some metrics for the student.

The current value stream map lays out the classroom learning process by flow as if walking in the shoes of the student and indicating the impact on the metrics for each process step, ending with the assignment to the teacher advisor program. If a metric changes between process steps, that is highlighted as such. Some metrics may remain unchanged between steps. There are several metrics on this current state map including GPA, Course Attendance, Skills, Prior Knowledge, School Attitude and External Factors. The selection of metrics is based on what matters to the stakeholder and the school identifies these items as key indicators of success after conducting a study with at risk student focus groups and by examining research for best practice.

In addition, along the bottom of the value stream map a timeline is set up against each process step and that is cross referenced to a scale measuring the student's propensity for failure based on the classroom learning process. Notice that the timeline for the current state is 64 weeks from course selection to completion of the teacher advisor program. There is considerable time of 24 weeks between course selection and course attendance. In contrast, there is minimal time of 50 minutes between initial course attendance and initial attitude and behavior adjustments. Also note the 20-week teacher advisor program following the course failure at the end of the process.

Start reading the value stream map at the upper right corner beginning with the student selection of the class, Process Step A, "Selects Class," and ending with Process Step F, "Course Failure/Teacher Advisor Program Begins." In that area, you will see the relationship of suppliers to the customer and to the process indicated along with supplier benchmarks.

A complete value stream mapping example based on the high school teacher advisor program presented in Chapter One is described next. As a reminder, this advisor program was first examined by the superintendent and building administrators through the Lean Essentials introduced in Chapter One, the five why's and overproduction. Now the district wishes to examine the teacher advisor program more closely and uses the Lean Essentials introduced in this chapter, value stream mapping and learning to see waste, to do so. A description of how the value stream map is built follows.

The current state value stream map of the teacher advisor program is created so that employees engaged in improving the process of the teacher can accomplish the following:

1. To agree on who the stakeholder is and who suppliers are;
2. To see the process the stakeholder experiences;
3. To measure the stakeholder's experiences and final result;
4. To look for ways to improve the process by eliminating waste and creating value;
5. To create an improved future state.

Study the current state value stream map for these results. Take a moment and examine the map as present reality from the view point of the at risk student. As you examine this value stream map, you may "see waste." This is the point of value stream mapping; learning to see waste is a desirable cognition.

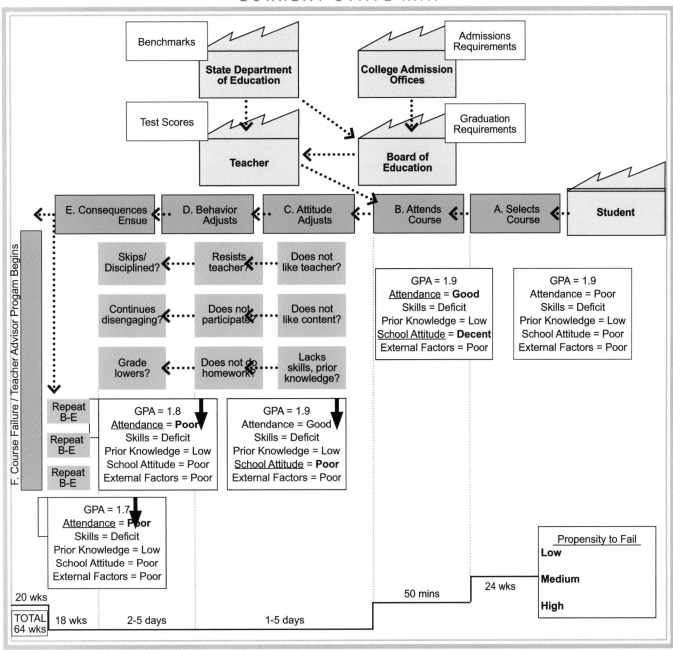

In the current state value stream map, there are four points of improvement, represented by kaizen bursts, that become apparent. These kaizen bursts, representing new ways of seeing the teacher advisor program and re-conceptualizing how to make the program more effective, are described next. These kaizen bursts appear on the next diagram, as overlays to the previous Current State Value Stream Map.

For the first kaizen burst, between Process Step A, "Selects Class," there is considerable lead time, 24 weeks, and many data points, student indicators of at-risk status, prior to the student's Process Step B, "Attends Class." This tells the school that before the student sets foot in the class there is a chance to prepare the student for the class, rather than intervene after the failure. The metrics for the average at risk student the school selected indicate that a lack of prior knowledge, the lack of skills, the negative impact of external factors, are malleable factors to varying degrees. The ability to identify the data for students at the point of class selection and to introduce preparation programming for the class in the weeks preceding the class represent a significant shift in the current allocation of resources and effort of the current teacher advisor program. At this point in the process, the at risk student is at a medium level of propensity to fail.

For the second kaizen burst, it is critical to monitor the quality of the first class experience because by the end of that initial 50-minute time period, the student is moving toward success or failure already. The propensity to fail increases greatly during this 50-minute period, a short but critical stage. Hence, after Process Step B, "Attends Class," immediate follow-up to the initial first class interaction may greatly increase the chance of class success.

For the third kaizen burst, monitoring of any repetitive negative behavior for Process Steps B-E is also important. In the event of a problem, this will require real time intervention and a highly communicative process between the classroom teacher and the student. Propensity to fail remains high with this combination of variables. However, it is noticed that if prevention work is carried out in real time to create positive adjustments to the interaction of Process Step C, "Attitude Adjusts," and Process Step D, "Behavior Adjusts," this could be valuable for the at risk student.

For the fourth kaizen burst, the current state map now provides clarity on the need to shift the teacher advisor program from a full intervention effort to a blended preparation/prevention/intervention initiative. This, of course, infers the need for a different teacher advisor program design, requiring a reallocation of resources and effort, and more real time customized delivery of services. The kaizen bursts on the current state value stream map are represented below on the next diagram. This is followed by a new future state value stream map, incorporating the improvements from the kaizen bursts overlaid on the current state map.

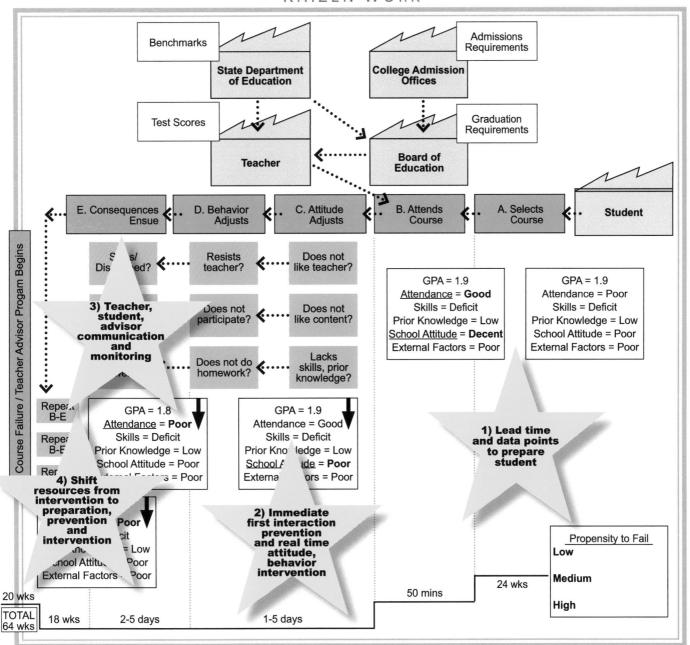

The school next creates a **value stream map** of the desired future state based on the kaizen bursts. The future state **value stream map** is below.

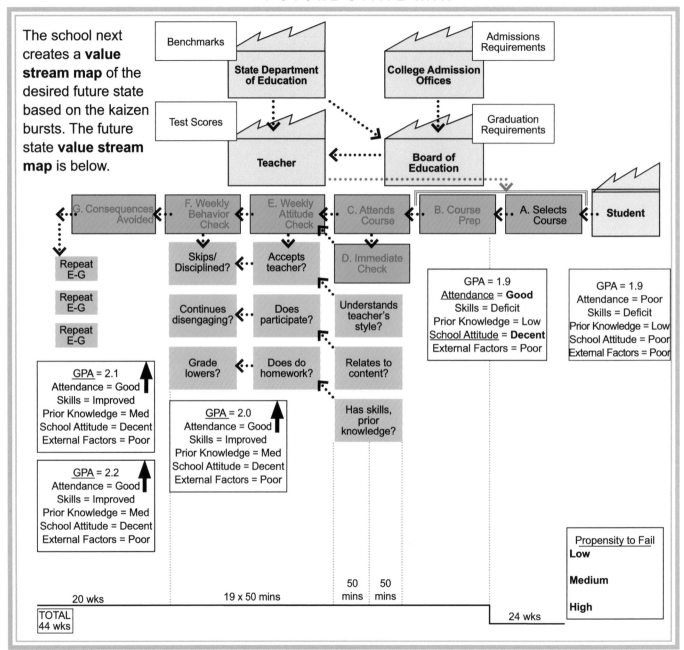

The school next creates a value stream map of the desired future state based on the kaizen bursts. The future state value stream map is on the left page.

The future state value stream map completely refashions the teacher advisor program. The total timeline for the engagement is now reduced from 64 weeks to 44 weeks by front loading a preparation program, which is included in the 44-week total. This preparation effort is intended to produce improved student metrics up front. The new teacher advisor program also provides an immediate check as real time intervention after the first class to maintain the student's metric from the preparation stage. The weekly behavior and attitude check further provides real time intervention with the goal of continuing to improve the student's metrics. Upon course completion, the teacher advisor program terminates.

By using the Lean Essentials, the lean tool of value stream mapping in three stages of the current state, kaizen work, and future state, and the lean concept of learning to see waste, the school leader is able to foster continuous improvement of a current system. It is always easier to design and deploy a new system, rather than redesign and redeploy a current system. But, since most schools do not have the luxury of starting with a blank slate, a new system, this combination of value stream mapping and learning to see waste as a system operates does open up new possibilities for managing organizational change and driving to improvement.

Critical Attributes of the Tool: Value Stream Mapping

- Use the tool for improvement work.
- Use the tool based on mission, vision and key stakeholders.
- Use the tool for a shared understanding of the current state versus the future state and the transition issues between the two.

Critical Attributes of the Concept: Learning to See Waste

- Use mental and emotional discipline to see waste (and value) by associating with the stakeholder.
- Learning to see waste (and value) challenges the current condition.
- Use learning to see waste (and value) in order to bridge the gaps between reality and desired mission/vision.

Leadership Coaching:

To begin using Value Stream Mapping and Learning to See:

1. Select a key process that directly impacts your stakeholders as identified in your mission/vision.
2. Obtain stakeholders' data and facts regarding their process experiences.
3. Identify key metrics for value stream measurement.
4. Honestly map out the current state of the process with metrics.
5. Look for value and waste on the value stream map using kaizen.
6. Identify what you corporately "see" on the current state map with kaizen bursts.
7. Create a future state map increasing value and decreasing waste.
8. Set up a transition plan to move from the current to future states.
9. Assign the process improvement work to a task force with clear deliverables, standards, assessments, and structure.

CHAPTER 3

Concept: Plan-Do-Check-Adjust Improvement Activity
Tool: The A3

THE CONCEPT:
Plan-Do-
Check-Adjust

LEAN
ESSENTIALS

THE TOOL:
The A3

In 1902 the artist, Auguste Rodin, sculpted a bronze and marble depiction of a man deep in reflection, a famous piece known as *The Thinker*. This sculpture has been cast many times over and used in various settings to remind people of the power of philosophical and critical thought. While history has had its plethora of great thinkers, Rodin captured the value of substantive contemplation and created an image that has endured. Such an image has become increasingly important in the information age whereby work is understood more and more as inquiry and the development of knowledge.

During that same era, the early 1900's, and in great contrast to the symbolism of *The Thinker*, the Second Industrial Revolution occurred in the United States and popularized a method of creating products known as mass production. The use of motorized assembly lines was introduced, where products were transported to workers at stations to complete repetitive, sequential work. The value of this method of production was that it created substantial efficiency which meant that increasing numbers of products became affordable to more consumers. While history provides several longstanding examples of workers employed in mass production, the image of the factory worker engaged in the Motorized Assembly Line captures the epitome of current societal values of what work looks like—industrious activity based on metric-driven performance.

School leaders engaging their districts in continuous improvement may be surprised to learn that they will find all the help they need in implementing continuous improvement in the combined images of *The Thinker* and the Motorized Assembly Line. In fact, the Lean Essentials, the lean tool, the A3, and the lean concept, the Plan-Do-Check-Adjust cycle, enable leaders to unleash continuous improvement. To understand these Lean Essentials, an explanation of the Plan-Do-Check-Adjust concept is presented with a description of the A3 tool.

The Plan-Do-Check-Adjust concept, also called PDCA, is a four-step learning loop which spirals an organization into continuous improvement. Fundamentally, PDCA requires organizational activity to occur by design which falls into one of two categories. The first category, reminiscent of *The Thinker*, but scaled to a corporate, rather than an individual scale, is Organizational Intelligence. The second category, reflective of the Motorized Assembly Line on an organizational level, is Performance Management. The key to the concept of PDCA as continuous improvement is that Organizational Intelligence and Performance Management are linked together as follows.

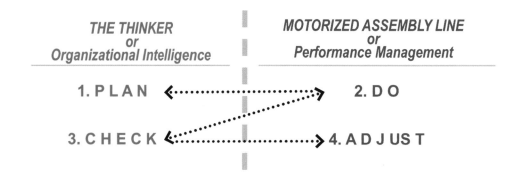

When using the PDCA concept, school leaders learn to focus on these two categories and create organizational participation in all four activity areas, eventually developing an organizational learning loop. So, as a first step in employing all four PDCA activities, there should be an understanding of what each activity area includes, allocation of human capital, social capital, or financial resources to those separate activity areas, and then directing protocols for connecting the four activities. Each of the four activity areas are described in detail next, Plan-Do-Check-Adjust, beginning with the Plan activity. Each element of the PDCA cycle is represented by the tool, the A3, as it depicts the PDCA concept.

A3	A visual management tool that describes corporate work in four activity groups: Planning, Doing, Checking and Adjusting as continuous improvement
PDCA	The Plan-Do-Check-Adjust (PDCA) cycle is a four stage routine that represents habits of mind and work that creates an organizational learning loop for continuous improvement

PLAN

The Plan activity, reflective of The Thinker, encumbers five elements:

- the identification of a theme for the project at hand,
- a critical overview of the background or setting,
- a current condition,
- a root cause analysis of the current condition, and
- a statement of the problem.

If Plan work is done well, it tends to ignite two synergizing dynamics. The first is the creation or enhancement of a vision focused on the best possible future, one that is clearly different from the current state. The second is the instigation of some tension stemming from dissatisfaction with the current state, now better understood as worthy of improvement. In other words, unless key stakeholders are riled up about an existing condition, improvements will not occur. The Plan activity precipitates the environment for improvement. Typically, school leaders must provide leadership in this activity area by creating organizational space for the Plan work to occur. This is done by allowing time to be allocated to the Plan activity and by rewarding and recognizing those who engage in it.

PLAN	Vision Matters

So, let's start with a scenario in which a superintendent has asked the special education director to reduce her budget by the equivalent of two positions for next year. The special education director, faced with this declining budget situation and the assumed reduction of two special education positions, decides to use the Lean Essentials, the A3 and the PDCA concept. In doing so, she chooses first to engage in Plan work. Instead of simply announcing the reduction of two positions based on seniority, the director uses this budget problem as a venue for examining the process of special education delivery more closely and instigating improvement. By using Plan work, the following scenario occurs under the auspice of the special education director, beginning with the selection of a Theme.

By carefully selecting the Theme for this Plan work and by shifting from the previous theme identified by the superintendent, the special education director is able to set the tone for her department. In the past when position reductions were imminent as first framed by the superintendent, the unstated Theme was "Let's Reduce and Announce A Two-Position Reduction Based on Seniority." Instead, knowing that budget goals can be met while improvement is implemented, she chooses a different Theme, "Let's Work To Eliminate Waste in Special education Delivery."

What is important about the selection of any Theme is that it overtly states precisely what is poised for action, instead of leaving that open for interpretation. The emotionality of position reductions, for instance, can create a lot of confusion within various stakeholder groups. While everyone may not be in favor of the Theme stated in this Plan activity, at least they know what it is and have the opportunity to suggest or negotiate changes to it. Without the outright publicized selection of a Theme, a lot of meetings, phone calls, sidebars, and mudslinging can bog down the real work of getting to a final decision that benefits the district. In other words, by stating the Theme, organizational transparency is evident.

So, the director calls a one-hour meeting with her department to describe the Theme and to explain the Plan activity that will ensue. First, the department is challenged with the task of considering the "customer" under this Theme. They also discuss the alignment of this Theme with the district's mission. The department decides that the four customers are: 1)special needs students, who derive value from instructional improvement support and 2) special education administrators, faculty and staff, who derive value from process improvement and possible job preservation. The Theme was changed to "Let's Understand and Eliminate Waste in Special Education Delivery to Improve Instructional Value." The A3's Theme is written out and the meeting is dismissed.

A3 - PLAN **Theme:**	Representing the scope and focus of the work in the scenario as: *Let's Understand and Eliminate Waste in Special Education Delivery to Improve Instructional Value*
PDCA Thinking	The Theme is the first element of PLAN activity

For the next element of the Plan activity, the special education director calls a second one-hour meeting and asks her department to outline the traditional approaches taken for budget/position reductions. This is the development of the Background element. The department discusses their past experiences with budget/position reductions and comments are captured on a flip chart. They next depict the old process by using a spaghetti diagram indicating the myriad of steps and interactions between stakeholders required to execute a solution. The spaghetti diagram is so full of lines and arrows, that there is not much white space appearing on the diagram. There is a dialogue about the effectiveness and efficiencies of the traditional process, and the consensus is that the previous budget reduction process did not work that well, which, in turn, impacted the quality of the final decisions made. A discussion about the scope, quality and impact of past decisions occurs and the director asks her department to consider the net results of those decisions against the selected Theme for this Plan work. Those comments are captured on a flip chart. The meeting is summarized by reviewing the Background element now completed, including the list of comments on the employees' perspective of the traditional process, the spaghetti diagram of this process and the analysis of the deliverables of the previous process against the Theme. The special education director then asks the department to contemplate what a more effective and efficient process for budget reduction might look like using the Theme, "Understanding and Eliminating Waste in Special Education Delivery to Improve Instructional Value," for the next meeting.

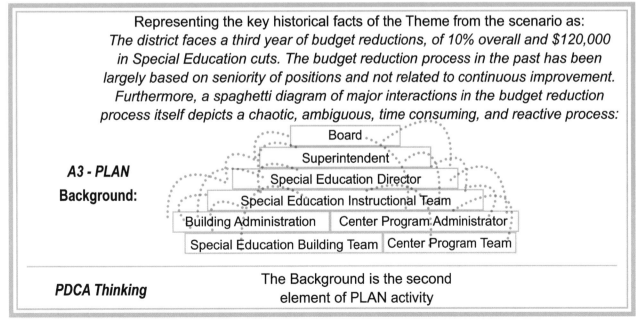

Representing the key historical facts of the Theme from the scenario as:
The district faces a third year of budget reductions, of 10% overall and $120,000 in Special Education cuts. The budget reduction process in the past has been largely based on seniority of positions and not related to continuous improvement. Furthermore, a spaghetti diagram of major interactions in the budget reduction process itself depicts a chaotic, ambiguous, time consuming, and reactive process:

A3 - PLAN

Background:

| Board |
| Superintendent |
| Special Education Director |
| Special Education Instructional Team |
| Building Administration | Center Program Administrator |
| Special Education Building Team | Center Program Team |

PDCA Thinking

The Background is the second element of PLAN activity

A third two-hour meeting is called to examine the Current Condition of special education delivery in the district and its impact on the budget/position reduction situation. The department gathers and creates a value stream map of the current state of special education delivery, with the special education student/parent as the customer and the special education department, building principals and general education teachers, paraprofessionals and area service agency centers as the suppliers. The metrics selected are based on FTE's or Full-Time Equivalent positions required to complete the various tasks required--activities such as student testing, Response-to-Intervention programming, Individualized Education Plan development and monitoring, the myriad of student support venues, and instructional delivery platforms. The department then examines this value stream map to identify points in need of improvement and points of waste. A list of these the points are generated. The department then revisits the Theme by discussing the relevance of the improvement list to it. Comments and concerns are solicited and then sorted out by consensus of the department as to which improvements on the list related to the Theme and which did not. The director summarizes the Relevant Points of Improvement List and discusses the implications of those improvements for the budget reduction and position reduction problem. The meeting is dismissed.

A3 - PLAN **Current State** **Relevant Points of Improvement for Special Education**	Represented as an honest understanding of the present reality in the scenario as: *Current Budget-Related Savings* *Points of Process Improvement:* • *$5000: Paperwork redundancy in referrals, evaluation process* • *$5000: Communication gaps in family relationship management* • *$20000: Poor RTI design* • *$10000: Poor early intervention* • *$10000: Poor student data management for instructional program improvement*
PDCA Thinking	The Current State is the third element of PLAN activity

38

A fourth one-hour meeting is called by the director to analyze with the department the root causes of the Relevant Points of Improvement. At this meeting, the department is divided into small groups with a faciliator and each group selects one Relevant Point of Improvement to examine for thirty minutes. The task of these small groups is to use the lean tool, the Five Why's, in order to determine the root cause of the current condition of the point of improvement. As the department splits into teams, the Relevant Points of Improvement are examined with one group member serving as the facilitator and asking the "why's" of the small group. For example, one Relevant Points of Improvement item involved the need to improve the student data for the allocation of Response-to-Intervention (RtI) programming. When the small group facilitator continued asking her group why this problem existed, the conversation evolved from:

- *This starts with the problem being that the data capture for the RtI program for students was limited. The facilitator asks, "Why?"*
- *to "The data collection system is poorly designed."*
  The facilitator asks "Why?"
- *to "The teachers don't know what data is needed." The facilitator asks, "Why?"*
- *to "We have not told the teachers what data is needed." The facilitator asks, "Why?"*
- *to "There is not a clear decision making process or communication protocol in place." The facilitator asks, "Is this the root cause?"*
- *to "Yes."*

The use of the Five Why's in this small group, for example, steers the work that proceeds from this analysis. So, this group then discusses how to shift the focus from not making the work that follows focused on the first cause, the limited data capture but, rather on the last cause, correcting the decision making process and communication protocol. In terms of budget allocation, this root cause analysis using the Five Why's represents a shift in the allocation of dollars for expanding the data capture capabilities by purchasing different software, for example, to the allocation of human capital for designing and streamlining a decision making process and communication protocol.

After thirty minutes each group reports out on the root cause of the Relevant Points of Improvement as a series of Statements of the Problem. These statements are recorded and summarized and the meeting is dismissed with the understanding that the Director will seek the Superintendent's approval of this list in order to meet the budget reduction needs.

A3 - PLAN **Statements of the** **Problem**	Representing needs-based statements emanating from root cause analyses in the scenario • *$5000 waste: Paperwork redundancy in referrals,* *evaluation process—* ***Need for clear protocols, standards*** • *$5000 waste: Communication gaps in family* *relationship management* ***Need for shared ideas and skills*** • *$20000 waste: Poor RTI design* ***Need for grade level coordination*** • *$10000 waste: Poor early intervention* ***Need for student metrics*** • $10000 waste: Poor student data management for instructional program improvement ***Need for building/classroom level data***
PDCA Thinking	The Current State is the fourth element of PLAN activity

The Plan activity represents a total of five hours of active participation meetings, each involving some preparation by the director and interaction with the superintendent. What the director has accomplished in these four meetings is quite substantial in terms of developing Organizational Intelligence for this problem. Within her department, there is an understood Theme, a shared description of the Background, a statement of the Current Condition and a Root Cause Analysis, and a concise set of Statements of the Problem.

The director reports back to the superintendent on the progress made with the budget reduction mandate and indicates what the Relevant Points of Improvement and Root Cause Analyses revealed about the special education delivery system in the district. The total savings through process improvement came to $50,000 of the $120,000 needed for reduction. She shares the visual management tools used to conduct the Plan activity, for example, the spaghetti diagram, feedback on past budget/position reduction processes, the value stream map and kaizen of the current state of the special education delivery system. The superintendent examines the Statements of the Problem and concurs with this list. Together, they create a prioritized list of the most pressing Statements of the Problem in regard to the reduction of the budget. Instead of eliminating two teaching positions *outright, the superintendent and director see that part of the budget reduction dollars can come from process improvement and the elimination of waste and then they can ascertain where teaching position reductions must occur. However, prior to the execution of improvement work, which will take place next as Do activity, the superintendent and director confirm the following budget reduction list of $50,000 in process improvements, resulting in some non-teacher position reductions and other changes, and the remaining $70,000 in outright teaching position reductions as follows:*

$5,000 waste: Paperwork redundancy in referrals, evaluation process—
      Need for clear protocols, standards
            In house process improvement
            Reduction of "fixing of paperwork" position
            .25 administrative assistant position reduction

$5,000 waste: Communication gaps in family relationship management
      Need for shared ideas and skills on school/family partnerships
            In-house development via visual management/lean tools, learning, coaching
            Reduction of "phone call/message taker" position
            .4 clerical position reduction

$20,000 waste: Poor RtI design
      Need for grade level coordination
            In-house redesign with Special Education Instructional Team/Teachers
            Reduction of "instructional coordination" position
            .4 special needs coordination position reduction

$10,000 waste: Poor early intervention
      Need for student metrics
            In house IT dashboard development/teacher training with instructional side
            Reduction of software vendor costs
            50% vendor contract reduction

$10,000 waste: Poor student data management for instructional program improvement
      Need for building/classroom level data
            In house IT dashboard development/teacher training with instructional side
            Reduction of software vendor costs
            75% vendor contract reduction

$70,000 in remaining FTE teacher position reductions

Following this session, the superintendent distributes to the board, to the director and her department, and to the building and center administrators the completed Plan section of the A3 for discussion at the next district administrative meeting. The director is instructed to continue with the Do work next.

DO

The Do activity, represented by the Motorized Assembly Line metaphor, includes two components:

- the statement of a target condition for the work, and
- an implementation chart, including duties, timelines, etc.

If Do work is done well, it tends to create team focus in two ways. The first way is through overt clarification of shared measures of performance by a statement of the Target Condition. The second way is through the clarification of roles and responsibilities, allocation of power, and accountability in the Implementation Chart. In contrast to the Plan activity, which is exploratory in nature, Do activity is directional. In other words, Do work is highly purposeful because the goal is understood as a shared solution to a problem or set of problems, rather than an isolated, perfunctory series of steps. And, Do activity specifies the actual work to be done, so that participants are clear about Performance Management. When Do work takes places, employees understand not only what is at stake, but why it matters and how to do the work. The Do activity, therefore, is essentially the core improvement work, achieving deliberately higher target condition than the current state and accomplishing that with less waste. Typically, school leaders must enable and empower teams to function at high levels of optimization in this activity area by defining success openly and facilitating that outcome. This is done by endorsing Plan activity which springboards to the Do Target Condition and allowing necessary resources to be allocated to the Implementation Chart, even if it means exploiting other resources to make sure the work gets done.

DO	Productivity Matters

So, let's continue to follow the superintendent's revised charge to the special education director to reduce her budget by the equivalent of $50,000 in process improvements and $70,000 in teacher reductions for next year. To review, the Plan work described in the previous section ended with the most highly prioritized Statements of the Problem driving to the following:

A3 - DO **Target Condition:**	Represented as the benchmarks of performance as a metric of root cause solutions. Enact budget reductions totaling $120,000 with $50,000 in improved effectiveness and efficiency of Special Education Delivery processes and $70,000 in teaching reductions to meet standards of adequacy funding.
PDCA Thinking	The Target Condition is the first element of DO activity

The Target Condition is actionable, measurable, and has the potential to be scalable in future years or for other areas of district operation. The Target Condition, as the proceeding step to solving the Statements of the Problem, is the congruent activity to the preceding Plan activity. It is essential that the Theme, Background, Current Condition and Statements of the Problem drive to the Target Condition, to activate the potential for a continuous improvement process in Special Education Delivery. As the full enactment of the Lean Essentials, the PDCA concept and the A3 tool unfolds, the superintendent intends to garner benefits for the district, even in the midst of difficult budget reductions.

After discussing the Target Condition with the board and the administrative team, the superintendent asks the director to prepare an Implementation Chart. The director sits down and composes the Implementation Chart, calls a 90-minute meeting to present it to her department for discussion, refinement and endorsement, and then brings it back to the superintendent.

The superintendent examines the Implementation Chart with the director and accepts it. The superintendent is interested in setting up Do work surrounding the reduction of budget that enhances the district by eliminating waste in the special education delivery processes and by working to create added value for the customers of these processes (students, parents, teachers, building administrators). While these may seem like dichotomous results to have in mind—eliminate waste and create value—by relying on the PDCA concept and utilizing the A3 tool to visually represent what is underway and accomplished, he will be able to attain both.

The superintendent discusses the Implementation Chart with the board and the administrative team. He then asks building administrators to conduct school/program meetings to describe what Do activity will occur, so that all stakeholders understand both the Plan and Do work. The following Implementation Chart is published as a part of the A3, along with the entire Plan and Do sections presented earlier.

A3 - DO Implementation Chart	Representing the work plan of duties, deadlines, shared measures of performance and other data to clarify roles, responsibilities, standards and deliverables of the process improvement for the scenario as:				
	PROCESS IMPROVEMENT	**DUTIES/TOOLS**	**DUE**	**METRICS**	**SAVINGS**
	Referral Process-protocols/standards	Stakeholders to redesign process/ Value Stream Map Kaizen CX Analysis Poka Yoke Work	2 WKS	Efficient Effective Consistent Understandable Defect free	$2,500
	Evaluation Process-protocols/standards	Stakeholders to redesign process/ Value Stream Map Kaizen CX Analysis Poka Yoke Work	2 WKS	Efficient Effective Consistent Easy Defect free	$2,500
	School/Family Partnerships-ideas/skills	Stakeholders to redesign process/ CX Analysis Train stakeholders/ Skill Development	2 WKS 20 WKS	Effective Relevant Valuable Applicable Interactive Fun	$5,000
	RTI-grade coordination	Stakeholders to redesign process/ Process Map CX Analysis	5 WKS	Effective Consistent Embedded	$20,000
	Early Intervention-metrics driven	Stakeholders to identify metrics/ Value stream map IT redesign/ Train teachers Reduce contract	2 WKS 3 WKS 10WKS 1 WK	Efficient Effective Accessible Efficient Easy	$10,000
	Student Data-achievement driven	Building, classroom stakeholders to identify data needs/ Gap analysis Process map Train teachers Reduce contract	10 WKS 10WKS 1 WK	Researched Best practice Customized Easy	$10,000
	FTE Reductions	Individual meetings Issue paperwork Job relocation help	3 WKS	Respectful Helpful	$70,000
PDCA Thinking	The Implementation Chart is the second element of DO activity				

The Do activity is approved by the superintendent and begins immediately. The superintendent instructs the director to set out the next activity area, Check activity, as the Implementation Chart is enacted.

CHECK

The Check activity, represented by The Thinker symbol, is designed to ensure that the Target Condition is met. It allows for mistakes to be identified and problems to be solved as a way to foster the elimination of waste through two components:

- the triangulation of three or more concise Methods of Assessment or Auditing and
- shortfalls against metrics

When Check work is carried out, it catapults teams into the improvement cycle in two ways through the development of enhanced Organizational Intelligence. The first way it facilitates continuous improvement is by providing an embedded platform for fostering a culture of emotional and professional safety so that feedback is accurately reported and not whitewashed. The second way it drives continuous improvement is by guaranteeing that feedback loops to critical stakeholders are operational.

The Check activity is the stepping stone to systems thinking for teams. It steers the direction of the work into a learning loop as it creates the interaction needed to relate work that is done to some measure of value. It also causes a team to reconsider the customer again and why the work is done. The Check activity keeps employees from getting too caught up in what they produce by providing a culturally acceptable way to examine how they produce it and the impact of those efforts. In other words, the Check activity requires the team to review not only the quality of deliverables, but the quality of standards, protocols, actions and ideas as interrelated elements as specified in the Do activity.

So, let's continue to follow the superintendent's use of the PDCA concept and the A3 tool related to the Check activity.

Upon approval of the Do Implementation Chart presented previously for the Plan Theme, "Let's Understand and Eliminate Waste in Special Education Delivery to Improve Instructional Value," the superintendent requests that the director and her department clearly identify the Methods of Assessment or Auditing to uncover the Shortfalls. The director calls a one hour department meeting to review the approved Implementation Chart and to ask the team to outline the Check activity. The department breaks again into small groups based on the seven tasks on the Implementation Chart and establishes the Methods of Assessment or Auditing and the Shortfalls. As the Methods of Assessment or Auditing are actually completed in the future, the Shortfalls will be noted then. It is too soon to lay this out at this point since the work has not commenced. The director presents the proposed Check activity to the superintendent and they discuss it. The superintendent concurs with the Check activities and they are formalized. The following table is added to the A3 tool.

A3 - CHECK Methods of Assessment, Audit and Shortfalls	Representing the examination of the DO work using data and facts to make sure that productivity has occurred in the scenario as:			
	PROCESS	*TARGET*	*ASSESSMENT / AUDIT*	*SHORTFALL*
	Referral Process- protocols/standards	$2,500 Consistent Understandable Accessible Defect free	Position reduction -Observe process -Audit mistakes -Interview, survey -Shadow students	
	Evaluation Process- protocols/standards	$2,500 Consistent Easy Accessible Defect free	Position reduction -Observe process -Audit mistakes -Interview, survey -Shadow students	
	School/Family Partnerships- ideas/skills	$5,000 Relevant Valuable Applicable Interactive	Observe events -Review communiqués -Interview , survey -Assess training	
	RTI- grade coordination	$20,000 Effective Consistent Embedded	Vendor contract -Observe process -Student data -Interview, survey -Shadow students	
	Early Intervention- metrics driven	$10,000 Effective Accessible Efficient Easy	Vendor contract -Observe process -Student data -Interview , survey -Shadow students	
	Student Data- achievement driven	$10,000 Researched Customized Easy	Vendor contract -Teacher observation -Student data -Interview, survey	
	FTE Reductions	$70,000 Respectful Helpful	Position reductions -Job placement -Climate survey	
PDCA Concept	The Assessment, Audit, Shortfall Chart is the one element of CHECK activity			

Although the Check activity will unfold as the Do work occurs, the superintendent wants to include this in the A3 tool early on, so that the district does not neglect to complete it. It is easy to forget or to run out of time to engage in the Check activity, so setting this out now represents the superintendent's commitment to maintaining the budget reduction process as a continuous improvement initiative. And that leads to the last element of the PDCA concept and the last section of the A3 tool, the Adjust activity.

ADJUST

The Adjust activity, in the Performance Management category, finalizing the Motorized Assembly Line metaphor, and completing the first full roll of the continuous improvement cycle. It includes two elements,

- reflections on specific improvements required for a better outcome and
- brief documentation of those changes.

When Adjust work is carried out, it formalizes organizational learning for better Performance Management in two ways. First, it promotes total quality management by describing organizational learnings for ongoing and future work. Second, it promotes both rapid development and rapid deployment for the future and allows the organization to progress forward from the previous improvement cycle.

The Adjust cycle is the capstone element for driving continuous improvement to the Target Condition to an even better future state. It causes the team to overtly pinpoint and implement changes with shared understanding. In other words, the Adjust activity provides the opportunity to get to optimal performance levels by not "reinventing the wheel." It is a second chance to eliminate waste and create value, hence it provides all involved with the project to reflect, internalize and implement improvement. Adjust activity is action-oriented.

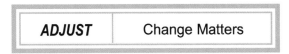

So, let's continue to follow the superintendent's use of the PDCA concept and the A3 tool related to the Adjust activity. After carrying out the Check Methods of Assessment or Auditing and the Shortfalls, Adjust Reflections and Documentation are created. The following is an example of what the superintendent and director might encounter.

After completing the Check activity following the implementation of the Do work, the director solicits via email Adjust Reflections and Documentation from her team. These are compiled and reviewed at a one hour meeting. The final A3 is then prepared and sent to the team via email for approval. Once presented to the superintendent, the Adjust changes are implemented.

A3 - ADJUST Reflections	Representing the final step of continuous improvement work where learning is examined and new changes are documented based on CHECK work in the scenario as: *What did we learn to do better?*
A3 - ADJUST Change Documentation	*What changes were made as a result of our learning?*
PDCA Thinking	The Reflections and Change Documentation are the two elements of the ADJUST activity.

The Adjust activity helps the district to look at what worked and what did not work, to apply those key revelations forward, and to manage changes so that the initiative remains sustainable. A failure to engage Adjust activity will short change the potential developed. Enacting Adjust activity will complete the first full revolution of continuous improvement. For school leaders, Adjust activity is a great organizational tool because it enables risk taking associated with change management to occur in a safe environment. Adjust activity makes change a predictable, but not predominate, element of work.

THE A3 TOOL

The A3 is a useful visual management tool for various district stakeholders, especially all vertical and lateral reports, at all stages of the project. The A3 goes through two stages, a work in progress A3 and a final A3. As a working document, the A3, is shared and posted, and may not be cosmetically appealing. But, the point of all of this is not to produce the document per se, but rather to enact the PDCA concept widely via the A3 tool.

While the A3 can be used widely, it is particularly useful during the work-in-progress stage to

the superintendent in:
- serving as the lean leader
- providing strategic decision making and approval
- facilitating a culture of readiness
- ensuring good communication

the special education director in:
- scoping the initiative
- facilitating the initiative as continuous improvement
- overseeing and guiding team learning

the special education departmental team in:
- analyzing problems
- designing solutions
- improving processes
- gaining a system's perspective
- measuring and defining success

the building level administrators, teachers in:
- understanding the initiative
- contributing to the initiative
- deploying the processes
- checking results

the board of education in:
- approving overall resource allocation
- understanding the improved process

Depending on the initiative at hand, the district may also decide to make the A3 available to the community, for example, students, parents, and others, or to those who serve in Assessment/Audit and Shortfall work, such as participants in focus groups, interviews, surveys, and such. Often the final A3 is a good summary of improvement work that the enterprise benefits from having access to.

As the project is deployed, the A3 is posted on the district's wiki as a work in progress. As changes are made, those are recorded on the wiki documentation. Once the project is debriefed, the final A3 will be posted for access by the district's stakeholders. The work in progress A3 is posted to the wiki, based on the PDCA work previously described in this chapter as follows.

A3: SPECIAL ED BUDGET REDUCTION/IMPROVEMENT

PLAN / THEME:
Let's Understand and Eliminate Waste in Special Education Delivery to Improve Instructional Value

PLAN / BACKGROUND:
The district faces a third year of budget reductions, of 10% overall and $120,000 in Special Education cuts. The budget reduction process in the past has been largely based on seniority of positions and not related to continuous improvement. Furthermore, a spaghetti diagram of major interactions in the budget reduction process itself depicts a chaotic, ambiguous, time consuming, and reactive process

PLAN / CURRENT STATE:
Relevant Points of Improvement

Current Budget-Related Savings
Points of Process Improvement:
- *$5000: Paperwork redundancy in referrals, evaluation process*
- *$5000: Communication gaps in family relationship management*
- *$20000: Poor RTI design*
- *$10000: Poor early intervention*
- *$10000: Poor student data management for instructional program improvement*

PLAN / STATEMENTS OF THE PROBLEM:
- *$5000 waste: Paperwork redundancy in referrals, evaluation process—*
  Need for clear protocols, standards
- *$5000 waste: Communication gaps in family relationship management*
  Need for shared ideas and skills
- *$20000 waste: Poor RTI design*
  Need for grade level coordination
- *$10000 waste: Poor early intervention*
  Need for student metrics
- *$10000 waste: Poor student data management for instructional program improvement*
  Need for building/classroom level data

DO / TARGET CONDITION:
Enact budget reductions totaling $120,000 with $50,000 in improved effectiveness and efficiency of Special Education Delivery processes and $70,000 in teaching reductions to meet standards of adequacy funding.

DO / IMPLEMENTATION CHART AND CHECK:

Process / Due / Duties / Tools	Metrics / Savings	Check / Assessment Short Falls
Referrals-process/standards 2 WKS /Stakeholders to redesign process/Value Stream Map, Kaizen, CX Analysis, Poke Yoke	Consistent User friendly Defect free/ $2,500	- Position reduction - Observe process - Audit mistakes - Shadow students
Evaluation-process/standards 2 WKS /Stakeholders to redesign process/ Value Stream Map, Kaizen, CX Analysis, Poke Yoke	Consistent Accessible Defect free/ $2,500	- Position reduction - Observe process - Audit mistakes - Interview, survey
School/Family Partnerships-skills 2 WKS/Stakeholders to redesign process/CX Analysis 20 WKS /Train stakeholders/Skill Gap	Relevant Interactive Fun/ $5,000	- Observe events - Review communiqués - Assess training
RTI-Grade Coordination-process 5 WKS/ Stakeholders to redesign process/Process Map, CX Analysis	Effective Embedded/ $20,000	- Vendor contract - Observe process - Student data
Early Intervention-metrics driven 2 WKS/Stakeholders to identify metrics/Value stream map 4 WKS/IT redesign/ Reduce contract/ Building, classroom stakeholders to identify data needs/ Gap analysis,Process map 10 WKS/Train teachers	Efficient Effective Accessible Easy Researched Best practice Customized $10,000	- Vendor contract - Observe process - Student data - Interview , survey - Shadow students
Student Data-achievement driven 10 WKS/Building, classroom stakeholders to identify data needs/ Gap analysis, Process map 10WKS/Train teachers 1WK/Reduce vendor contract	Researched Best practice Customized Easy/ $10,000	- Vendor contract - Teacher observation - Student data - Interview, survey - Shadow students
FTE Reductions 3WKS/Individual mtgs/Issue paperwork,Job relocation help	Respectful Helpful/ $70,000	- FTE reductions - Job placement - Climate survey

ADJUST/ Reflections and Change Documentation:
- What did we learn to do better?
- What changes were made as a result of our learning?

By using the Lean Essentials, the A3 tool and PCDA concept, the superintendent and special education director have ushered the special education budget reduction process into continuous improvement work. This proves to be significantly different leadership work than utilizing the previously mapped out budget reduction process. The old process was rife with lots of wandering exchanges of information and dispositions; a final, and often disconnected, examination of the budget shortfalls; and emotional decision making to eliminate positions, not to mention, the stressful work of dealing with the aftermath of the old process. The PCDA concept enables the superintendent, the special education director, her team, and key stakeholders to foster a healthy culture of change management, even when faced with the difficulty of budget reduction. It also presents a cleaner budget reduction process with a purpose that is superior to the simple elimination of positions.

For the district to successfully marry continuous improvement to budget reduction, all four elements of the PCDA concept require activity. Each element has its benefits in terms of staging the organization for the next step. Table 3.1 indicates how these elements are interrelated and summarizes the distinctions between the PCDA elements described above. More importantly, it illustrates how all four elements require representation in organizational work if it is to be deemed to be continuous improvement.

This is an important point for school leaders to consider, because some of these elements may be more difficult than others for a leader to enact, depending on leadership style and state of organizational readiness. Typically, organizations have an innate propensity or cultural disposition to specialize in one of these four quadrants of activity. If this natural condition is left alone, it will inhibit continuous improvement. Hence, any PCDA element executed in isolation falls short of continuous improvement as the following four examples illustrate.

ADJUST				D. Change Matters
CHECK			C. Accountability Matters	
DO		B. Productivity Matters		
PLAN	A. Vision Matters			
	PLAN	*DO*	*CHECK*	*ADJUST*

Table 3.1. Isolated A3 Elements, A-D, as Organizational Culture

Example A / Vision Matters: Districts specializing in PLAN activity have good strategic plans and tend to have high levels of awareness of best practice. However, when PLAN activity is not connected to DO activity and there is a lack of tactical ability to execute the strategy. Because of this, employees can become disenfranchised from the organization's purpose and even disregard best practice as just "talk."

In contrast, when using the Lean Essentials, the A3 tool and the PDCA concept, PLAN activity drives to a Root Cause Analysis and Statement of the Problem, an application of strategy and best practice to critical thinking, not just organizational tolerance. In other words, PLAN activity overcomes the problem of having lots of good conceptual ideas on an abstract level with no pragmatic sense of what to do on a practical level. An example of a Vision Matters only organization is a district that promotes the importance of technology literacy in a vision statement, but does not understand why there is a lack of technology literacy in the district, cannot state the root cause of this current state, nor understand how to change it.

Table 3.2 below illustrates how the PDCA concept expands organizational capacity in this regard, as a driver to the other A3 elements, indicated by activities E, G, and I. So, if your district has a propensity for PLAN activity, then use that as a driver to the rest of the PDCA concept.

ADJUST	I.	Strategy Drives Modifications
CHECK	G.	Strategy Drives Monitoring
DO	E.	Strategy Drives Tactics
PLAN	A.	Vision Matters
		PLAN

Table 3.2. Connecting PLAN Activity to A3 Elements

Example B / Productivity Matters: Districts specializing in DO activity work hard and tend to meet deadlines and compliance guidelines well. However, when DO activity is not connected to CHECK activity, there is a lack of purpose in the work and the district will not be able to implement total quality management. Because of this, employees can become stressed and burned out from the pace and lack of purpose.

In contrast, when using the Lean Essentials, the A3 tool and the PDCA concept, DO activity drives to a Target Condition with the supporting Implementation Chart, an application of activity focused by shared measures of performance and clear accountability, not just organizational busyness. In other words, DO activity overcomes the problem of having lots of highly skilled and hardworking people engage on a reactive level with little sense as to what improvement differences will be gained by doing so. An example of a Productivity Matters only organization is a district that promotes the importance of completing a curriculum alignment initiative over the summer, without clarity on what the future state of the curriculum specifically should look like and what roles, responsibilities, and timelines are needed to meet this future state.

Table 3.3 below illustrates how the PDCA mental model expands organizational capacity in this regard capacity in this regard, as a driver to the other A3 elements, indicated by activities F, K, and M. So, if your district has a propensity for DO activity, then use that as a driver to the rest of the PDCA concept.

ADJUST	M.	Tactics Drive Modifications
CHECK	K.	Tactics Drives Monitoring
DO	B.	Productivity Matters
PLAN	F.	Tactics Drive Stategy
		DO

Table 3.3. Connecting DO Activity to A3 Elements

Example C / Accountability Matters: Districts specializing in CHECK activity monitor work through structures and procedures and tend to examine decisions carefully. However, when CHECK activity is not connected to ADJUST activity, there is a tendency to create layers of bureaucracy and policy to regulate work in a meaningless way and the district's purpose gets lost in the layers of the maze. Because of this, employees can become very territorial, protective or competitive as they learn to "work around the system" to complete their duties.

In contrast, when using the Lean Essentials, the A3 tool and the PDCA concept, CHECK activity drives to an Assessment/Audit Plan with the accompanying identification of Shortfalls, an application of activity focused by organizational learning in order to improve the ongoing or next execution, not just looking for mistakes as organizational blaming. In other words, CHECK activity overcomes the problem of having lots of resources devoted to monitoring work that gets done with little sense as to what improvement differences will be gained by doing so. An example of an Accountability Matters only organization is a district that creates an instructional administrative position to redo or fix poorly delivered instruction after high student failure rates occur, without improving the teacher hiring, induction, training and evaluation systems to avoid these shortfalls in the first place.

Table 3.4 below illustrates how the PDCA concept expands organizational capacity in this regard capacity in this regard, as a driver to the other A3 elements, indicated by activities H, L, and O. So, if your district has a propensity for CHECK activity, then use that as a driver to the rest of the PDCA concept.

ADJUST	O.	Monitoring Drives Modifications
CHECK	C.	Accountability Matters
DO	L.	Monitoring Drives Tactics
PLAN	H.	Monitoring Drives Strategy
		CHECK

Table 3.4. Connecting CHECK Activity to A3 Elements

Example D / Change Matters: Districts specializing in ADJUST activity are interested in doing things differently from a previous sequence and tend to be willing to pioneer new initiatives. However, when ADJUST activity is not connected back to PLAN activity, there is a lack of facilitation of change as a process and change is viewed as an event or a revolving door of irrelevant leadership philosophy. Because of this, employees can become steeled against new ideas and initiatives and think of any change as the latest phase or flavor of the month which will pass quickly.

In contrast, when using the Lean Essentials, the A3 tool and the PDCA concept, ADJUST activity sets up Reflections and Change Documentation, the development of organizational praxis by debriefing and identifying what is useful to carry forward and what still needs to be changed, rather than reinventing the initiative each time. In other words, ADJUST activity is a second chance for improvement and a first chance at sustainability. An example of a Change Matters only organization is a district that offers comprehensive staff development training in the newest trends, such as new software products, reading programs, or instructional methods with no comprehensive strategy for organizational adoption.

Table 3.5 below illustrates how the PDCA concept expands organizational capacity in this regard capacity in this regard, as a driver to the other A3 elements, indicated by activities J, N, and P. So, if your district has a propensity for ADJUST activity, then use that as a driver to the rest of the PDCA concept.

ADJUST	D.	Change Matters
CHECK	P.	Modifications Drive Monitoring
DO	L.	Modifications Drive Tactics
PLAN	H.	Modifications Drive Strategy
		ADJUST

Table 3.5. Connecting ADJUST Activity to A3 Elements

The power of the A3 tool and the PDCA concept lies in synergy of synchronous drivers of powerful organizational work that are triggered when these activities commence. Consider the how the District's capacity for continuous improvement is enhanced when the dynamics of Tables 3.2-3.5 are combined into a system as represented in Chart 3.1 below.

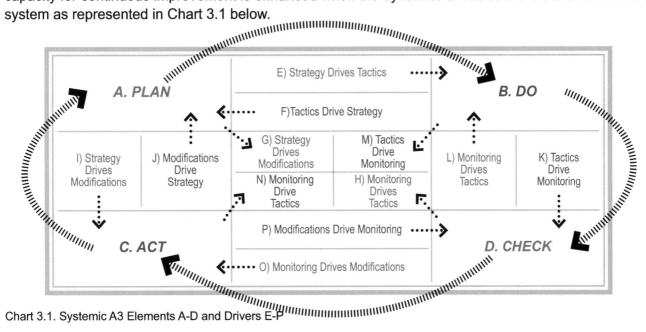

Chart 3.1. Systemic A3 Elements A-D and Drivers E-P

So, in some ways the simplicity of the PDCA concept if understood as a checklist of sequential work is appropriate. However, there is more to grasp here in terms of understanding how the PDCA concept can truly impact your school district. That is, when the A3 tool is fully employed, it is much more than a linear progression of work; it is a fully developed system of organizational work, where each element of the PDCA concept represents a mutual interaction of activity.

Keep in mind the metaphor of Rodin's The Thinker and the symbol of the Motorized Assembly Line as equally valuable areas of organizational work of Organizational Intelligence and Performance Management. By balancing PDCA activity, both forms of work occur in the best possible way, with better results, improved processes and positive morale. The more congruent organizational thinking and organizational doing are overall, the closer to success and sustainability initiatives will be. This is why the Lean Essentials, the A3 tool and the PDCA concept, can be so useful for schools.

So, Plan activity not only drives to Do activity, but it sets up an interaction that interconnects Organizational Intelligence to Performance Management—and Performance Management back to Organizational Intelligence. Subsequently, Do activity not only drives to Check activity, but it sets up an interaction that interconnects Performance Management to Organizational Intelligence—and Organizational Intelligence back to Performance Management. In addition, Check activity not only drives to Adjust activity, but it sets up an interaction that interconnects Organizational Intelligence to Performance Management—and Performance Management back to Organizational Intelligence. And finally, Adjust activity not only drives to Plan activity, but it sets up an interaction that interconnects Performance Management to Organizational Intelligence—and Organizational Intelligence to Performance Management.

A3	An organizational tool that describes work as: Plan-Do-Check-Adjust
PDCA	A system of organizational thinking and doing of interrelated elements that ensures continuous improvement will be planned for and executed

The point is that there is always something better driving organizational thinking and doing under this lean tool, the A3, and concept, Plan-Do-Check-Adjust. So, this set of Lean Essentials provides the essence of what continuous improvement is and the process needed to implement it. School leaders are in a position to set up these dynamics for their districts, where the best of both worlds, The Thinker and the Motorized Assembly Line, the premium Organizational Intelligence and the highest quality Performance Management, are realized. No matter how difficult the challenges at hand, the A3 tool and the PDCA concept can be invaluable for school leaders.

Critical Attributes of the Tool: The A3

- Use the tool within the context of corporate inquiry and problem solving to promote continuous improvement.
- Make it honest.
- Use inclusive, but deliberate, protocols for stakeholder involvement.

Critical Attributes of the Concept: PDCA

- Use the mental model of creating congruence between The Thinker and The Motorized Assembly Line.

Allocate time and resources for four forms of work, PDCA.

- Use the PDCA concept to acquire vision, productivity, accountability and change.

Leadership Coaching:

To begin using the A3 and PDCA Cycle:

1. Start with a need or painful problem and scope it out.
2. Start the PDCA cycle at any point, just complete the learning loop.
3. Optimize the visual management attributes of the A3 tool and PDCA concept by considering your communication plan and stakeholder roles.
4. Use A3 and PDCA to increase stakeholder involvement and organizational transparency.
5. Understand what each stage of the PDCA cycle provides and manage resources to accomplish those ends.

CHAPTER 4

The Concept: Zero Defect Thinking
The Tool: Kaizen

THE CONCEPT:
Zero Defect
Thinking

LEAN
ESSENTIALS

THE TOOL:
Kaizen

So far, three key Lean Essentials and tools have been presented. To review, Chapter 1 described a high school remediation program used to reach at-risk students. Chapter 1 detailed how a superintendent used the Lean Essentials, the Five Why's tool to prompt learning conversations and to identify the concept, finding overproduction. Chapter 2 further developed the theme of extending instructional leadership to continuous improvement. Chapter 2 described how the Superintendent and administrators from Chapter 1 enabled instructional process improvement using the Lean Essentials, the tool of value stream mapping and learning to see waste. This shifted resources to prevention of student failure, rather than to remediation of student failure. Chapter 3 outlined a method for fiscal management based on continuous improvement methods and subsequent better use of scarce resources. Chapter 3 described how a special education director and superintendent managed to improve special education delivery by using the Lean Essentials, the A3 tool and Plan-Do-Check-Adjust concept to address budget reduction issues and implement improvements simultaneously.

Inherent in these three chapters is the ever present idea that one or more aspects of organizational culture, systems, processes, standards or routines will be observed, critiqued, improved and benchmarked as prompted by Lean Essentials. In this chapter a new set of Lean Essentials, a lean tool called kaizen and a lean concept called zero defect thinking, is presented to provide more insight into how to observe, critique, improve and benchmark to get positive results.

Kaizen, a lean tool, was briefly presented in Chapter 2 as an icon on the value stream map, a "burst" of enlightenment. In this chapter, kaizen is examined in detail and illustrated as a useful lean tool, particularly when it is coupled with the lean concept, zero defect thinking.

Kaizen represents two stages of action. It literally means to take apart (kai) and then to put back together (zen). Hence, kaizen occurs as Stage One, dismantling, and as Stage Two, improving. Stages One and Two are actual organizational events. Therefore, when employing the kaizen tool, it is typical to use the term kaizen event indicating application of the tool. Depending on which system or process is going through a kaizen event, Stages One and Two may take five minutes to several days to complete. Kaizen events are also either singular or periodic, or both, ranging from 'daily huddles' by teams to quickly assess small points of dysfunction, to 'shark attacks' of cross functional groups to solve a present and constraining problem, to 'a blitz' of entire departments or organizations examining every core process for improvement. Regardless of the kaizen event and the time allocated or the people involved, kaizen always occurs in Stage One and Stage Two.

Zero defect thinking is the concept that drives the Stage One and Stage Two kaizen event. Zero defect thinking refers to the elimination of waste to a level of tolerance represented by excellence and the highest quality possible—where one can say that a particular process or service has been improved to the point of "zero defect" status. Zero defect thinking also occurs in two stages, Stage One, as data driven auditing for defects, and Stage Two, as data driven benchmarking against improvement. Stage One zero defect thinking poses the challenge, "What is wrong with the current process?" Stage Two zero defect thinking sets up the promise, "What can we achieve?" The standards of zero defect thinking are to make sure that problems are not created, accepted or passed along. So, as work occurs that is subject to zero defect thinking, one examines the work as a process and questions, "Are there defects in this process that I am creating?," "Are there defects in this process that I am accepting?" and "Are there defects in this work that I am passing along?"

KAIZEN	An organizational tool that occurs as a quick meeting, single event or extensive event that enables critical conversations to occur so that defects are not created, accepted or passed along.
ZERO DEFECT THINKING	A critical analysis process whereby questioning the quality of a solution occurs to eliminate errors and waste.

The state of zero defect status is uncovered when the standards of zero defect thinking are addressed collectively through kaizen events. So, the combination of daily huddles, shark attacks or the kaizen blitz with the standards of zero defect thinking to not create, accept, or pass along problems, is a powerful work-embedded strategy in the pursuit of perfection. The culture of kaizen and zero defect thinking occurs with disciplined thinking and organizational cultures that enable employees to act when the standards of creating, accepting and or passing along defects are violated.

The diagram below, Figure 4.1, illustrates how Stage One zero defect thinking drives Stage One kaizen. And further, how Stage Two zero defect thinking drives Stage Two kaizen. As a lean leader, it is critical to carry out both stages of zero defect thinking and kaizen work. Otherwise, it is impossible to obtain improvement.

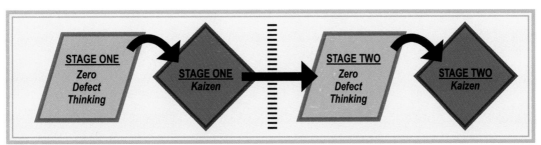

Figure 4.1 - Stage One and Stage Two Kaizen

Basically, these two stages of kaizen rely on data to formulate and culminate zero defect thinking. Data is used as input to start Stage One and as output to complete Stage Two. Data driven decision making in Stages One and Two are represented by the diamonds in Figure 4.2 below. A complete picture of data-driven decision making to formulate and to finalize kaizen solutions is represented by the relationships of the parallelograms and the diamonds as indicated in Figure 4.2.

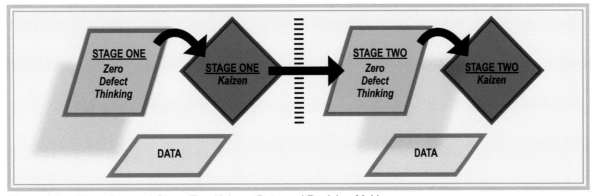

Figure 4.2 – Stage One and Stage Two Kaizen, Data and Decision Making

What the Lean Essentials, kaizen and zero defect thinking entail, is a complete system comprised of Stages One and Two. This system matters because if school improvement is limited to the general context of Stage One zero defect thinking and kaizen, positive results are impossible to realize. For example, Stage One of zero defect thinking occurs when you look at achievement data that falls short of strategic goals and you experience a rapid and general understanding that there are problems to address in the instructional system. Since Stage One kaizen is driven by Stage One zero defect thinking, work commences to address the instructional system or elements of the system that are dysfunctional and to dismantle them. This may include replacing curriculum or student assessment systems or even removing people, for example. Needless to say, using only Stage One zero defect thinking and kaizen is a sure way to create a toxic culture. Stage One should produce a helpful audit of data that exposes waste in order to clarify what process or system needs to be dismantled. As indicated in Figure 4.3, that Stage One not the end of kaizen and zero defect thinking.

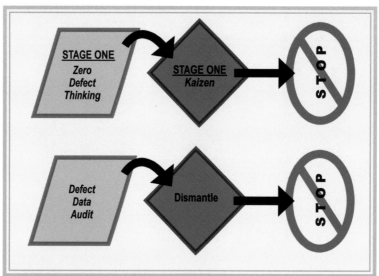

Figure 4.3 - Stage One Only as Non-Kaizen

When Stage Two zero defect thinking and kaizen do not occur subsequent to Stage One, people are often on edge, feeling like they are expected to operate at levels of perfection that are unrealistic and unsupported. Stopping at Stage One means that complete solutions are not provided for when shortfalls are in evidence. Under such dynamics, zero defect thinking often melds into 'zero defect exposure.' This means that employees may put substantial effort into hiding information in order to protect themselves, instead of developing improvement solutions. Organizations stuck in Stage One zero defect thinking and kaizen find that employees may become non-participatory in improvement work because contributing to the auditing of data for system defects only provides evidence of problems with no hope of resolution. Stage One zero defect thinking and kaizen is often translated to employees as "Run for cover!" In other words, there is no benefit in finding shortfalls and in taking a system apart unless it results in progress. So, if you begin with Stage One, then you must commit to Stage Two as well.

Let's look at how this might work. Assume that your district has data indicating that a subgroup of students have fallen behind academically. Under Stage One only, zero defect thinking is used when examining the information. These data can drive kaizen, 'taking apart the system,' resulting in some form of dismantling, such as the removal of inadequate curriculum, or even, in some cases, the removal of underperforming administrators or teachers. This is common with crisis management where emergency financial management or receivership is occuring. So, it is obvious in this example that Stage Two zero defect thinking and kaizen are needed. Otherwise, the system is left dismantled with no curricular, teaching or administrative improvements. And if curriculum, teachers, or administrators are the focus of the blame in Stage One instead of a focus on process improvement, then there are no guarantees that the new curriculum, teachers, or new administrators will be better than the previous ones were. The dismantling of a system that occurs in Stage One must be linked to improvement in Stage Two.

Therefore, the process of dismantling in Stage One as a stand alone activity is purely destructive and is not considered improvement work unless Stage Two occurs. This is because engaging in Stage Two zero defect thinking and kaizen requires identifying a new benchmark of performance and adding into the system a different or revised curriculum, better trained teachers, or more prepared administrators in order to attain those metrics as indicated in Figure 4.4.

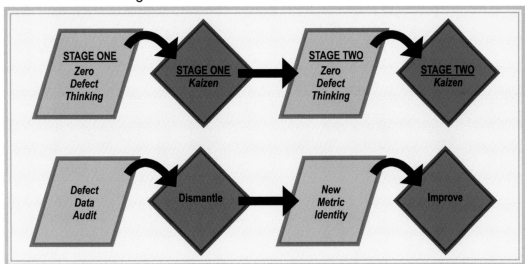

Figure 4.4 – Stage One and Stage Two Kaizen Data Management

Keep in mind that when lean is properly implemented, the emphasis is on respecting people, rather than on blaming, replacing or firing them. It is concerned also with improving processes, rather than on leaving them in states of dysfunction. In fact, firing people when metrics are not reached is often the opposite of using zero defect thinking and kaizen. And as pointed out here, Stage One kaizen as an isolated act, is not a part of lean leadership practice. The emphasis on process improvement and on respect for people requires the completion of Stages One and Two kaizen based on zero defect thinking. This is the foundation of lean leadership. So, let's consider what it means to be a lean school leader using the Lean Essentials of both stages of zero defect thinking and kaizen based in good data management practices.

The Lean Essentials, Stage One and Stage Two kaizen and zero defect thinking, are carried out as an improvement process embedded in data driven decision making. This is because Stage One zero defect thinking focuses on eliminating errors, mistakes and problems using an audit of some data set from one or more sources, such as action research, qualitative research or quantitative research. These data highlight an aspect of dysfunction as a response to zero defect thinking or "what is wrong" with the current process. Districts often have many data sets, such as poor graduation rates for student subgroups, high levels of parent complaints regarding cafeteria food, or increasing costs for computer repairs, for example, that can be highlighted in Stage One kaizen and zero defect thinking.

If data triangulation is done in the Stage One defect data audit, the more informative results regarding the defect or dysfunction may be. For instance, graduation rates when coupled with longitudinal student achievement data are more informative than graduation rates alone. Parent complaints, student surveys of food quality, and cafeteria morale information are more helpful as triangulated data than parent complaint data are in isolation. Annual technology budget comparisons, surveys of student/teacher usage, and comparisons of per pupil textbook versus e-book charges examined simultaneously are more useful than the technology repair budget data alone. In addition, if only Stage One dismantling is slated to occur in isolation, then in depth auditing and additional triangulation makes little difference. Because Stage One dismantling as a singular act is not the approach of lean leaders, using data to manipulate the outcome of dismantling is a hollow exercise. If both Stage One and Stage Two zero defect thinking and kaizen are intended, then best practice for assessing and auditing, such as triangulating data, is needed.

After Stage One zero defect thinking is complete based on a data defect audit, then it is easier to understand where dysfunction or waste are occurring for Stage One kaizen, dismantling. Stage One zero defect thinking and kaizen are centered on what is known as the "current state" of the process (or system) as indicated in

Figure 4.5. For instance, if Stage One zero defect thinking uncovers waste with some or all of the methods used in teaching reading, then it makes sense to dismantle those dysfunctional teaching strategies based on a solid understanding of the current state.

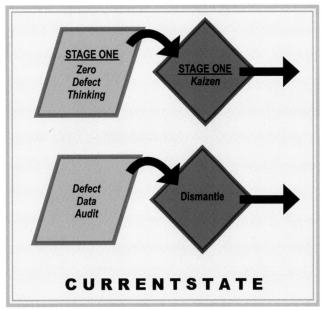

Figure 4.5 – Stage One Kaizen Current State

Stage One focuses on the current state. When Stage Two is deployed, the focus changes to the future state. In Stage Two zero defect thinking, data are used to identify new benchmarks of performance. These benchmarks should represent the level of tolerance the district can deliver to—once improvements are made. This means that zero defect thinking in Stage Two sets up new metrics based on what is attainable for a better future state. These metrics should not be randomly selected, but realistically identified by supposing that the old process or system is going to be changed. Stage Two kaizen follows, where improvements are implemented and the process or system is brought back with needed changes. These changes may be small incremental improvements or they may be large scale reform innovations. The work of Stage Two kaizen is framed around the new measures of performance derived from zero defect thinking for the desired future state as indicated in Figure 4.6.

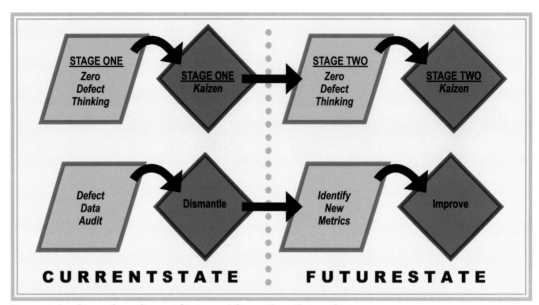

Figure 4.6 – Stage One, Current State, and Stage Two, Future State

The Lean Essentials, zero defect thinking and kaizen, require two stages of work: Stage One zero defect thinking that drives Stage One kaizen and Stage Two zero defect thinking that drives Stage Two kaizen. The data sets of zero defect thinking frame kaizen, relying on good data analysis to understand where defects in processes or systems are occurring in Stage One and then creating new metrics to ensure zero defect thinking endures in Stage Two. So, Stage One triangulation of the defect data audit is the input for zero defect thinking and for the decision making in Stage One kaizen. This means that decisions to dismantle what is not working are not emotionally driven or knee jerk reactions, but, rather, are conclusions from good data audits that drive judgments to improve current systems.

When Stage Two zero defect thinking and kaizen begin, data serve as output in the form of new benchmarking metrics. It is this second stage of work that fosters continuous improvement, brings process improvement to deployment, and ensures the fidelity of those improvements. Stage Two zero defect thinking is the key to this step because as new metrics of performance are selected, these data solidify Stage Two kaizen, to improve, not just to replace, the previous process. As Stage One is launched with data, the commitment to Stage Two is finalized with data. Data-driven and ensured decision making encompass continuous improvement as Stage One and Stage Two kaizen, developing higher levels of quality from current to future state—the most desirable result of all.

66

Next, let's walk through a comprehensive example of the Lean Essentials, Stages One and Two of the tool, kaizen, and the concept, zero defect thinking. The setting for this scenario stems from a national surge to change compensation structures for building principals from seniority-based to merit-based.

The superintendent of a large school district is wrestling with this issue since state and federal legislation has lifted the prohibition on tying administrative compensation to performance. The district's board has the expectation that the administrative compensation system aligns with these legislative changes. Since the impetus for this ban on the prohibition of merit-based compensation is founded in a set of tenets designed to drive school improvement to increase student achievement nationally and is aligned with the goals of the school district to do the same, the board and the superintendent reason that the issue warrants serious consideration. Therefore, the superintendent decides to utilize the Lean Essentials, the kaizen tool and zero defect thinking concepts, to assist her in revising the administrative evaluation system. She wants to avoid using only Stage One zero defect thinking and kaizen, a dismantling of the current system. Instead, she wants to run the improvement through a continuous improvement cycle based on a full kaizen process and zero defect thinking surrounded by triangulated data inputs and outputs. Navigating this change process using the lean tenets of demonstrating respect for people and deploying continuous improvement, in fact, requires the use of kaizen and zero defect thinking.

Using Stage One to examine the current state, zero defect thinking drives the kaizen process of defect data auditing. What is known about the current administrative evaluation system is that it is fairly open-ended, with building administrators being evaluated every three years by central office administrators. The process involves the central office administrator looking at student achievement scores and considering the central office adminstrator's impressions of the building administrator over time. Based on the student achievement data and the overall impression of the administrator, a central office administrator completes a checklist of leadership competencies and a supporting paragraph or two is added to the evaluation. Next, the building administrator reviews the document and then meets with the central office administrator to review it. Following the review, the document is signed by both parties and filed in the personnel office. It is possible for the administrator to file a waiver to not sign the evaluation or to file a grievance if warranted. It is also possible for the central office administrator to introduce a plan of improvement and ultimately to terminate the administrator if the evaluation indicates that performance is lacking.

This first pass at examining the current state of the administrator evaluation system indicates that the current process is full of problems. It clearly misses the benchmarks of a well-honed evaluation process. The building administrators don't like the evaluation process as it is not very informative or helpful in terms of professional development impact. The central office administrators don't like the evaluation process as it is not related directly to school improvement. The current process often proves to be a waste of time for both parties resulting in little impact on administrative professional growth or school improvement. With this setting as the background and current state, it is evident that the administrator evaluation system needs to be revised. Kaizen and zero defect thinking are the tools and concepts selected by the superintendent to move this initiative forward.

The superintendent prepares for the Stage One kaizen event by gathering longitudinal and triangulated data sets on student achievement, attendance, attitudes, development, retention/graduation, and post-graduate placements by building. She calls a meeting of central office directors and building principals and explains the background, setting and current condition of the administrator evaluation process. As the meeting participants look on wide-eyed, they are worried about what it might mean to improve the administrative evaluation process. The superintendent reassures them that they are going to work collectively on identifying a superb solution to the problems of the dysfunctional system.

So to start the Stage One kaizen and zero defect thinking off, the superintendent requests that these central office and building administrators volunteer to complete a defect data audit by core subject area teams of interest, Mathematics, Science, English Language Arts and Social Studies. In addition, she also requests that the administrative subject area teams set up and interpret the findings through the eyes of four key stakeholder groups: 1) the administrator being evaluated, and 2) the students, 3) the parents, and 4) the teachers that the administrator serves.

The superintendent describes the goal of this Stage One work carefully to the entire administrative team and they relax a bit, "The use of zero defect thinking in Stage One is to look for defects in the administrator evaluation process, not to single out people. The use of kaizen in Stage One is to dismantle the administrator evaluation process and is entered into with a commitment to complete Stage Two."

For Stage One zero defect thinking and kaizen to begin to contribute to continuous improvement, the superintendent asks for the defect data audit by four subject areas (Mathematics, Science, Language Arts, and Social Studies). Further for each subject area, reporting of the defect data audit is categorized by the four stakeholder groups: 1) the administrator, 2) the students, 3) the parents, and 4) the teachers. Through this defect data audit and zero defect thinking, a shared understanding is established of the current state of the administrator evaluation system's shortfalls.

As various building and central office administrators volunteer to contribute as team members to the data defect audit by subject area, the superintendent emphasizes that she is most interested in two criteria: a) the presence of triangulation of the data and b) the relevance of the data to the four key stakeholders, the administrator, the students, the parents and the teachers. The subject area defect data audit committees are given four weeks to complete their work.

The superintendent describes the rationale for this timeline to the committees, "Since kaizen is focused and succinct work, it should move along. We are not going to languish over this dysfunctional process, we are going to fix it using the structure of the Lean Essentials, the kaizen tool and the zero defect thinking concept. Stage One kaizen is our first step in ascertaining what we need to abandon or remove from our current administrative evaluation process, so I want you to use the defect data audit you conduct in your subject area committees to attack this system."

The four subject area committees plan to meet two times in the next four weeks. The purpose of the first meeting is to examine and triangulate the data sets. The purpose of the second meeting is to figure out where the problems are in the process and to recommend if additional data sets are needed in the future.

Five weeks later a meeting was called for the subject area administrative volunteers to present their analyses and interpretation findings in a way that highlights defects in the administrative evaluation system. Zero defect thinking is used by these committees to ask what is wrong with the current system using data sets available. The following explanation focuses on the findings of the mathematics team.

The mathematics team describe the data defect audit in relation to the administrative evaluation process. The data defect audit for mathematics revealed some interesting findings in relation to the four key stakeholder groups, the administrator, students, parents, and teachers. The mathematics team also divided their defect data findings further by Grades K-3, 4-5, 6-8 and 9-12.

The mathematics team identifies various data sets that measure value for the four stakeholder groups. They describe the current status of various data sets for the stakeholder groups to better understand what is wrong with the current system. The presence of quantitative and qualitative data and the need to triangulate for each stakeholder group in relation to the subject area of mathematics and the administrative evaluation process was uncovered as an area to dismantle.

As Figure 4.6 depicts, a simple force field analysis of levels of authority against levels of accountability showed that the current process is top heavy in terms of authority and accountability. In addition, the two data sets used currently, student achievement data and central office administrators' impressions, result in a problematic process flow. The mathematics team identifies key data sets currently available for the three key stakeholders and the data set coming from the impressions of central office administration. Finally, the data defect audit reveals the following problems. As outlined in Figure 4.6, the data sets are in various states

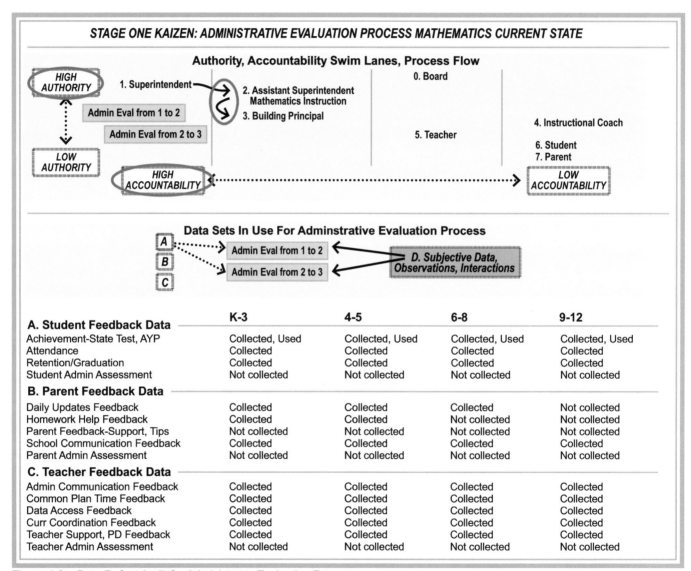

STAGE ONE KAIZEN: ADMINISTRATIVE EVALUATION PROCESS MATHEMATICS CURRENT STATE

Authority, Accountability Swim Lanes, Process Flow

Data Sets In Use For Adminstrative Evaluation Process

A. Student Feedback Data	K-3	4-5	6-8	9-12
Achievement-State Test, AYP	Collected, Used	Collected, Used	Collected, Used	Collected, Used
Attendance	Collected	Collected	Collected	Collected
Retention/Graduation	Collected	Collected	Collected	Collected
Student Admin Assessment	Not collected	Not collected	Not collected	Not collected
B. Parent Feedback Data				
Daily Updates Feedback	Collected	Collected	Collected	Not collected
Homework Help Feedback	Collected	Collected	Not collected	Not collected
Parent Feedback-Support, Tips	Not collected	Not collected	Not collected	Not collected
School Communication Feedback	Collected	Collected	Collected	Collected
Parent Admin Assessment	Not collected	Not collected	Not collected	Not collected
C. Teacher Feedback Data				
Admin Communication Feedback	Collected	Collected	Collected	Collected
Common Plan Time Feedback	Collected	Collected	Collected	Collected
Data Access Feedback	Collected	Collected	Collected	Collected
Curr Coordination Feedback	Collected	Collected	Collected	Collected
Teacher Support, PD Feedback	Collected	Collected	Collected	Collected
Teacher Admin Assessment	Not collected	Not collected	Not collected	Not collected

Figure 4.6 – Data Defect Audit for Administrator Evaluation Process

of collection and use. Figure 4.6 indicates by color coding the following states of collection and use: data collected was not being used effectively, what data might still need to be collected for triangulation, what data collected was being used effectively, and what data could be eliminated from the process.

This data defect analyis entailed an analysis of critical stakeholders and their information access and reporting needs based on authority and accountability. By adding process flow and a swim lane to the first half of Figure 4.6, the shortfalls in the administrator evaluation system are immediately apparent. In addition, the identification of current and needed data sets provides evidence that the data sets need revamping as well. There are many more data sets than are needed, yet some key data sets are missing.

The mathematics team then explains the implications for dismantling the administrative evaluation system based on the data defect audit. As they used zero defect thinking, they considered what constraints or problems were causing the system to malfunction. They asked, "What does the data defect audit tell us is causing mistakes, waste, dysfunction in the current evaluation system?"

They indicate that what they discovered was that the process is driven by those with high levels of authority and accountability in the district, yet this is not where the three stakeholder groups, key "customers" are in the current structure. This means that the current evaluation process distances these "customers." In fact, the team reports that these three stakeholder groups, the students, parents and teachers, are those with little or no authority or accountability in the current structure. So, there is a disassociation between serving the three stakeholder groups better via the process of administrator evaluation because of this structure that creates a distance barrier. In addition, the evaluation process does not associate the administrator with personal accountability for professional growth. In other words, the process does not drive value-added leadership development through self-reflection, self-planning or self-assessment.

The mathematics team also points out that the current administrative evaluation system is incorrectly driven by some loosely coupled subjective data, namely, the impressions formed by the administrator's interactions with central office. This stands in contrast to the objective data sets that the district has access to but does not use for the administrative evaluation, nor does it attempt to triangulate. It is noted that one exception to this is that one of the student achievement data sets are extremely influential in the administrative evaluation process. For this subject area committee, it was the mathematics achievement data that are influential.

The mathematics team highlights that the proposed entire student data set, the proposed entire

71

parent data set and the proposed entire teacher set are not triangulated nor used to evaluate building administrators. Furthermore, there are lots of data sets that are currently collected that are not used and other data sets that are not collected but should be. Overall, the mathematics team concludes that a lack of appropriate data collection technique and the lack of data triangulation are clearly missing.

The mathematics team summarizes that the Stage One kaizen data defect audit and zero defect thinking revealed these three points of dysfunction:

1. There is misalignment with the needs of key stakeholders: the administrator, the students, the parents, and the teachers under that administrator's auspice.
The protocols and structure of the evaluation process are misaligned with student, parent and teacher data sets and with professional accountability. Reflective and feedback protocols are non-existent, disallowing fostering and recognizing professional development of building administrators.

2. There is a lack of collection of critical data sets and/or data analyses.
Reliance on subjective data and student achievement data exclusively for building administrator evaluations is problematic in that there is a lack of appropriate data used, the data are not tied to the three stakeholder groups, and the data are not triangulated.

3. There is a lack of organizational meaning.
The current evaluation system is adrift from school improvement and propagates a perfunctory process that wastes time.

Since the mathematics team found these three defects by auditing the data used for administrator evaluation, they recommend dismantling the current system. This Stage One work is very informative as to exactly what needs to occur in Stage Two. Stage One highlights the need for Stage Two work which will restructure the purpose, culture and protocols of administrator evaluation. As described earlier, to dismantle this system in Stage One without a commitment to rebuild it in Stage Two, is not an option in kaizen. The remaining subject area teams for Science, English Language Arts and Social Studies reported similar findings and core problems. Consensus was as to defects in the administrative evaluation process was evident from Stage One work, Stage Two kaizen and zero defect thinking were next.

With Stage One completed, the superintendent tells the subject area teams that it is now time to focus on Stage Two, "From Stage One subject area committee work, we are poised to use the data defect audit to naturally flow into Stage Two. We know the specific problems within the current state because of the data defect audit. This sets up what needs to happen in Stage Two, creating improvements for the future state. You have identified the problems and now you will help to solve the problem as an administrative task force. Three subcommittees of volunteers will focus on these core problems. Just as with Stage One kaizen, Stage Two kaizen will move along. We are most interested in producing an improved administrator evaluation system that is relevant, effective and efficient, a system that creates value for all four key stakeholders, the administrator, students, parents, and teachers."

Through Stage One kaizen and zero defect thinking, it became evident to this administrative task force that the current system must be restructured in Stage Two. The Stage Two restructuring work is specified based on needs. These needs are: 1) the need to engage others with less authority who are key stakeholders and the need to increase accountability beyond central office, 2) the need to associate professional growth and school improvement with the process, to provide clear feedback and support protocols, and 3) the need to expand and triangulate data sets of key stakeholders. The picture that emerges from this Stage One zero defect thinking and kaizen indicates what is succinctly wrong with the evaluation system and what needs to occur in Stage Two kaizen. As described earlier, there are three key problems uncovered in Stage One kaizen that must be solved in Stage Two kaizen. To summarize, these problems with the current state of the evaluation system are: 1) a misalignment with the needs of key stakeholders, 2) a lack of collection of critical data sets and/or data analyses, and 3) a lack of organizational meaning. These three problems create the templates for the work of Stage Two.

With three core problems evident from Stage One kaizen, the superintendent then asks each subject area team to select three groups of two to four people to comprise the Stage Two Team, resulting in a series of three new subcommittees to address each of the three problems identified in Stage One. For Stage Two, the new core problem subcommittees are charged with working sequentially on each of the core problems, building of off or tailoring down each subcommittee's work. So, for Problem 1, the misalignment of administrator evaluation with the needs and input of key stakeholders, this first subcommittee is charged with solving Problem 1 and designing an improved future state for administrator evaluation using zero defect thinking and creating new metrics for the process. Once the Problem 1 subcommittee complete their work, they will hand the process improvement work to the next subcommittee for Problem 2, and so on. As each subcommittee completes its work, the results are posted as centralized documentation on a wiki for the next subcommittee. Formal and informal conversation is expected around each subcommittee's findings.

To assist the subcommittees in tackling the three core problems, the superintendent sets up a concept map and template for the three Stage Two subcommittees' activities. She explains that for Stage Two the use of zero defect thinking carries forward as the administrator evaluation process is reassembled in the future state. She also points out that the use of data changes from a defect audit of the current state in Stage One to the identification of new performance metrics in Stage Two.

For Stage Two kaizen, each subcommittee is expected to use four strategies. The first strategy (Strategy A) is to apply zero defect thinking to the core problem identified in Stage One in an effort to eradicate the problem. This is done by posing the question, "What defect is preventing the problem from being solved?" So, for example, for Problem 1 where the administrator evaluation process does not focus on the professional growth of the administrator or the key stakeholders the administrator serves (students, parents, teachers), Strategy A for zero defect thinking poses the question, "What is the defect that is preventing the administrator/ stakeholders (students, parents, teachers) from aligning with the administrator evaluation process?" So, for the administrators for example, the defect might be a lack of expectation to reflect, select, and self-assess on professional development goals. Strategy A attacks the defect.

The second strategy (Strategy B) is to create a remedy to the defect stated in Strategy A. The Problem 1 subcommittee response is to create remedies to those defects. So, for the administrators' lack of expectation to reflect, assess and improve, for instance, the remedy might be to create a leadership standards rubric against which self-reflection, goal selection, and self-assessment of written professional development plan is required. Strategy B creates a remedy for defect stated in Strategy A.

The third strategy (Strategy C) is to apply zero defect thinking to ensure that the remedy has no additional barriers that must be addressed. So the Problem 1 subcommittee asks, "What if the administrator is not honest or does not know how to reflect, self-assess, and plan effectively?" Then they would dive into that defect and address it by ensuring that the remedy works. They could suggest, for example, that training and templates should be provided to the administrator, that an internal mentor is assigned, and that the superintendent develops a safe culture for leadership development and self-assessment. Strategy C ensures that the remedy from Strategy B works.

The fourth strategy (Strategy D) is to identify new metrics that measure the improved process. The Problem 1 subcommittee, in addressing the core problem of lack of administrator involvement in the evaluation process, might recommend uses of data for benchmarking performance. For example, two benchmarks could be 100% evaluation process completion by the administrator with a mentor sign off and professional improvement on two measures (student, parent, teacher measures) per year with mentor sign off. Strategy D

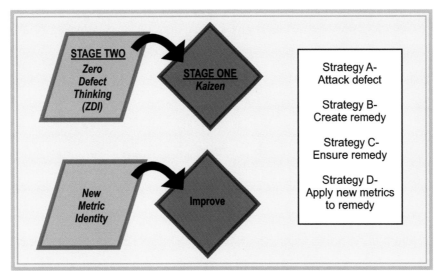

Zero Defect Thinking, Data Defect Assessment/Audit, Stage One Kaizen

Figure 4.7 - Stage Two Kaizen Strategies A-D Concept Map

applies metrics to the refined solutions from Strategies A-C. Figure 4.7 illustrates the templates for Strategies A-D that the subcommittees use. This depicts Strategies A-D in Stage Two kaizen and delineates Strategies A-C as embedded in zero defect thinking and Strategy D as embedded in new metric identification. These four strategies are protocols for bringing forth zero defect thinking through and through problem identification and problem solving. In the first steps of Stage One kaizen, data are used as inputs to uncover gaps in zero defect thinking. In Stage Two kaizen with Strategies A-D, data are used as outputs to ensure zero defect thinking is occurring.

The superintendent indicates that the following template for the three subcommittees is to be used to report and post findings on the wiki. Each subcommittee has four weeks to tackle their charges, with the expectation that this would require two ninety-minute meetings. Since Problem 1 is selected first, the subcommittee for Problem 1 completes their charge in the first four-week increment. Subcommittees for Problems 2 and 3 sequentially follow and build off of the work completed in prior four week increments. A chair for each subcommittee is appointed to facilitate the work. Figure 4.8 is the template the superintendent assigns to the four subcommittees to use for Strategies A-D in Stage Two kaizen.

STAGE TWO KAIZEN TEMPLATES FOR STRATEGIES A-D

STAGE TWO KAIZEN / Zero Defect Thinking/Strategy A / Attack the Defect

Stage One Kaizen Problem # Restated:

Gap Analysis Using Zero Defect Thinking:

*"What is the defect that is preventing ****?"*

GAP	GAP	GAP	GAP
Need to ****	Need to ****	Need to ****	Need to ****

STAGE TWO KAIZEN / Zero Defect Thinking / Strategy B / Create a Remedy

Problem # Remedy

REMEDY	REMEDY	REMEDY	REMEDY
Use ****	Use ****	Use ****	Use ****

STAGE TWO KAIZEN / Zero Defect Thinking / Strategy C-Ensure Remedy

Zero Defect Thinking Key Challenges

CHALLENGE	CHALLENGE	CHALLENGE	CHALLENGE
What if ****?	What if ****?	What if ****?	What if ****?

Zero Defect Thinking Key Assurances

Provide **** Set Up ****	Complete **** Test ****	Examine **** Pilot ****	Engage **** Solicit ****
Develop ****	Assist ****	Support ****	Record ****

STAGE TWO KAIZEN / Identity New Metrics / Strategy D-Create Metrics

Zero Defect Thinking Key Challenges

GAP	GAP	GAP	GAP
Metric Metric	Metric Metric	Metric Metric	Metric Metric

Figure 4.8 - Stage Two Kaizen Strategies A-D Templates

The Stage Two kaizen, using Strategies A-D, is completed for the Problem 1 subcommittee within four weeks. The subcommittee posts its templates on the wiki and uses an electronic forum for informal questions and discussions. After the four weeks' worth of Stage Two kaizen and zero defect thinking is completed, a meeting is called to summarize the work of the Problem 1 subcommittee and to review the online postings. It is also indicated that the Problem 2 subcommittee will commence. As that work begins, the Problem 2 subcommittee refers to the templates from Problem 1 subcommittee. The completed templates for the Problem 1 subcommittee are presented in Figures 4.9, 4.10, 4.11 and 4.12 below as posted on the wiki.

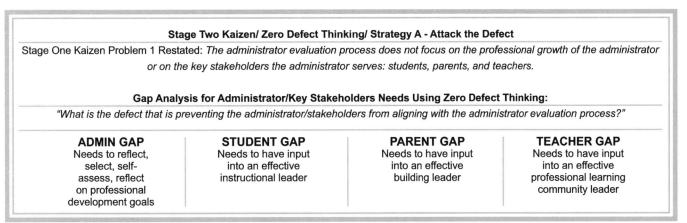

Figure 4.9 – Stage Two Kaizen Strategy A Zero Defect Thinking, Attack Defects

When the subcommittee prioritizes the key defects for Problem 1 with Strategy A, the gaps indicated above begin to aid in the formation of the basis of the Stage Two zero defect thinking and the new metric identification that will be a part of the new administrative evaluation system. The remedies proposed in Strategy B below are first round attempts at eliminating the defects in Strategy A.

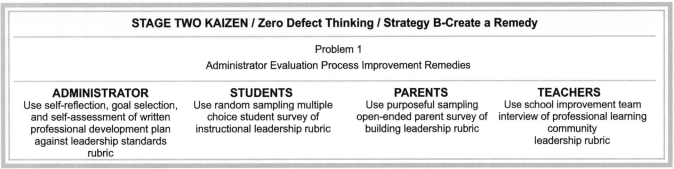

Figure 4.10 – Stage Two Kaizen Strategy B Zero Defect Thinking, Create a Remedy

In ascertaining remedies for the gaps indicated in Figure 4.9, the Problem 1 subcommittee selects Strategy B Remedies for Stage Two Kaizen. So, where a gap was identified regarding a lack of administrator, student, parent or teacher alignment with administrative evaluation, the Problem 1 subcommittee identified remedies for overcoming those gaps. For example, the gap regarding the need for administrators (those being evaluated) to align with the evaluation process through addressing the defect that prevents them from reflecting, selecting, self-assessing, and reflecting again on professional development goals, is remedied by the use of self-reflection, goal selection, and self-assessment in the form of a written professional development plan developed against a leadership standards rubric. In other words, the gaps in Stage Two Strategy A explicitly point out what the remedy should be.

The Problem 1 subcommittee also selects similar remedies for the remaining three stakeholder groups (students, parents and teachers) that were not aligned with the process yet, but should be based on the Stage One kaizen and zero defect thinking. Each remedy in Strategy A (Figure 4.10) involved designated stakeholder involvement (students/parents/teachers) with selected data collection devices to be evaluated against matching rubrics for instructional, building, and professional learning community leadership behaviors. Notice that these remedies are not open-ended solutions, where all students, teachers, parents complete a survey on the building administrator. Rather, there are selected stakeholders designated for involvement. Further, the data collection methods vary based on the stakeholder subgroups. In addition, the analyses of the data sets are based on rubrics for leadership standards. These remedies, therefore, are carefully tailored to solicit selected stakeholder subgroups with specific data collection tools against pre-determined standards.

Strategy C of the Stage 2 kaizen is used to further ensure that the Strategy B remedies work. Figure 4.11 below represents the zero defect thinking that the Problem 1 subcommittee invokes to make sure that the Strategy B remedies are deployed with success. In other words, for Strategy C the Problem 1 subcommittee considered the worst possible scenarios whereby the Strategy B Remedies might fail and indicate how to overcome those problems, resulting in Strategy C, zero defect thinking challenges and assurances.

Strategy C requires a deeper dive into zero defect thinking and a deeper remedy in order to drive the focus beyond the solution to the result. Some of the most highly regarded Strategy B remedies that the Problem 1 subcommittee put forth may not hold up well in the complexity and ambiguity of organizational life. Strategy C allows the Problem 1 subcommittee to recycle the solution through a second round of zero defect thinking. In doing so, the subcommittee looks at the remedies through the eyes of the stakeholders who will use them and thinks of what the biggest constraints to success are and how to ensure against those constraints. The information needed to engage in zero defect thinking key challenges and key assurances work can be carried out by a small pilot, interviews, or even informal conversations with these stakeholders as indicated in Figure 4.11.

STAGE TWO KAIZEN / Zero Defect Thinking / Strategy C-Ensure Remedy

Zero Defect Thinking Key Challenges

ADMINISTRATOR	STUDENTS	PARENTS	TEACHERS
What if the administrator is not honest or does not know how to reflect, self-assess, and plan effectively?	What if the survey questions are not valid or are confusing for instructional leadership?	What if the parent qualitative data set does not produce clear findings on state of building leadership?	What if the school improvement team sabotages the interview because of union concerns

Zero Defect Thinking Key Assurances

Provide training and templates for the process	Complete pilot testing for survey validity	Complete pilot testing for survey validity	Complete pilot testing for survey reliability
Set up internal mentoring to increase peer accountability	Test instructional leadership rubric for validity	Test building leadership rubric for validity	Set up letter of understanding with the union regarding survey purpose/process
Develop a safe culture of expectation of leadership development and self-assessment	Administer surveys to randomly selected classes with teacher, paraprofessional administration and support for students	Administer surveys using purposeful sampling to parent/teacher members via email with PTO support for participation	Administer a school improvement committee group interview using a question template facilitated by committee chair

Figure 4.11– Stage Two Kaizen Strategy C Zero Defect Thinking, Ensure Remedy

In Figure 4.11 above, Strategy C produces a list of key assurances or essential actions that the district must take for these remedies to work. In regard to Strategy B's remedy for the administrator, for example, Strategy C sets forth the key challenge. Namely, what if the administrator who is supposed to reflect, assess, and plan per Strategy B, does not know how to do this, does not know how to do this in the context of this district, or does not want to do it honestly? Strategy B is certainly a high stakes, high risk strategy for the administrator being evaluated. So there is a key challenge for the district as the administrator conducts an internal risk analysis. Questions, such as, "How do I self-reflect without setting myself up for failure or dismissal?" or "How do I know that this process is not punitive for me?" are key challenges to the success of Strategy B. If the administrator does not know what, how or why to engage in Strategy B, then there will be problems with timeliness, levels of engagement, levels of honesty, and so on. Strategy C boldly sets these key challenges out in the open based on zero defect thinking in an attempt to ensure success for Strategy B's remedies.

The Problem 1 subcommittee works through the key challenges and assurances in Strategy C for each stakeholder group and uses zero defect thinking to drill deeply into the potential constraints to success. Focusing on the administrator stakeholders, for example, the zero defect key challenges include concerns for honesty, as well as knowledge and competency development for self-assessment. To counter those key challenges, key assurances are developed. These key assurances serve as tactics to ensure that Strategy B works. For the administrator stakeholders, the Problem 1 subcommittee provides three key assurances to the key challenges. They include training, providing easy to use templates for the evaluation process, selecting an internal mentor with signoff responsibilities, and enhancing culture around the practice of self-assessment and observation. Each of these tactics provides a map as to how to engage administrators effectively in the evaluation process. Of course, each of the key assurances is subject to further zero defect thinking in the future. But, at some point, the district is going to have to enact this process. When it does so, it will continue to rely on the tenets of continuous improvement and apply a kaizen event with zero defect thinking around the deployment stage.

Strategies A-C assist the district partially through Stage Two kaizen and zero defect thinking. The last part of Stage Two kaizen, Strategy D, establishes the metrics and measures needed for this improved evaluation system. The specific benchmarks of performance needed from each stakeholder group to ensure successful Stage Two kaizen are called new metric identity. The new metrics ensure that data-driven decision making is enhanced for administrator evaluation, derived from objective and triangulated data sets. Stage One and Stage Two kaizen and zero defect thinking are completed when the metrics and measures of Strategy D are finalized.

> *Using the superintendent's template for Stage Two kaizen, Strategy D, the Problem 1 subcommittee identifies metrics for each stakeholder group. The new metrics are described as levels of participation or completion and are designed to ensure that the improvements in the administrator evaluation process are measured against meaningful benchmarks. Figure 4.12 below indicates two metrics for each stakeholder group. These metrics are designed to enhance the administrator evaluation process based on the previous stages of kaizen and zero defect thinking.*

> *Combining the findings from Stage One kaizen and the data defect audit and the findings from Stage Two kaizen, Strategy B, and zero defect thinking, the data sets previously collected and the new measures enhance opportunities for triangulation of objective data. The improved aspects of the*

administrator evaluation process include the potential for better data driven decision making in regard to responses such as leadership development or personnel intervention. Figure 4.12 below indicates measures providing a variety of data sets for the administrator's evaluation process.

STAGE TWO KAIZEN / Zero Defect Thinking / Strategy D Create Metrics

ADMINISTRATORS' METRICS	STUDENTS' METRICS	PARENTS' METRICS	TEACHERS' METRICS
100% process completion: Checklist with mentor sign off	80% survey participation: Use classroom procedures checklist with teacher sign off	30% survey participation: Work with PTO leadership to encourage participation	90% survey participation: Collect interview template from School Improvement Chair with signoff
Improvement on two *measures/year: Documented improvement on two measures with mentor sign off	Annual survey improvements: HR solicits survey improvements via email to teachers who administered student surveys	Annual survey improvements: HR solicits survey improvements via PTO Presidents who encouraged parent survey participation	Annual survey improvements: HR solicits survey improvements via email to School Improvement Chairs who facilitated teacher participation

*Measures for Administrative Evaluation:

I. STUDENT FEEDBACK DATA

Achievement Tests/AYP,	Previously Collected, Used
Attendance, Retention/Graduation	Previously Collected, Used
Student Admin Assessment—instructional leadership	Core Measure Previously Not Collected

II. PARENT FEEDBACK DATA

Daily Updates Feedback	Previously Collected
Homework Help Feedback	Previously Collected
Parent Feedback-Support, Tips	CoPreviously Not Collected
School Communication Feedback	Previously Collected
Parent Admin Assessment-building leadership	Core Measure Previously Not Collected

III. TEACHER FEEDBACK DATA

Admin Communication Feedback	Previously Collected
Common Plan Time Feedback	Previously Collected
Data Access Feedback	Previously Collected
Curriculum Coordination Feedback	Previously Collected
Teacher Support, PD Feedback	Previously Collected
Teacher Admin Assessment-professional leadership	Core Measure Previously Not Collected

Figure 4.12 – Stage Two Kaizen Strategy D Create New Metrics

Notice that for Strategy D, creating new metrics, that this response does overcome the problems with the lack of objective data sets and the lack of triangulation from Stage One. The new metrics are succinct, relevant and measurable. In addition, there are three categories (I-III) with various measures earmarked *for the* administrative evaluation process, including Student, Parent and Teacher Feedback data sets. This means that the administrative cohort now does have overtly identified benchmarks of performance for evaluative purposes and has multiple data sets from which to draw information. For example, for the administrative stakeholders, there are two metrics: 1) 100% process completion with mentor signoff and 2) improvement on two measures per year. This allows the administrator to focus on two items per year to improve based on data. In addition, the various tactics, such as providing an internal mentor, offering outcomes-based professional development training, and requiring action planning/reflecting are process improvements designed to support the administrator's improvement.

> *As the Problem 1 subcommittee reports out after four weeks and passes on its work to the Problems 2-3 subcommittees to complete Stage Two kaizen, the district is subsequently able to create a new administrative evaluation system that addressed the problems identified. Stage One kaizen work delineated problems with assessment and feedback protocols, reliance on subjective and non-triangulated data, and realignment of the authority and accountability culture of evaluation around key stakeholders. Stage Two kaizen work created solutions to the problems and worked to ensure that the solutions were durable. As the remaining Subcommittees complete their work, an improved administrative evaluation system is ready to pilot in the district.*

As Figure 4.13 below indicates, kaizen and zero defect thinking steered this improvement process with integrity. When the Stage One and Stage Two kaizen were completed, the superintendent and the administrative team had collectively torn down a perfunctory and wasteful process and recreated an improved process that was ready to test as a pilot. What had been accomplished using the concepts and tools of lean, zero defect thinking and kaizen, was a good shared understanding of the problems of the current state based on a data defect audit and the need for a clearly defined future state driven by performance and participation metric data. The intention of using kaizen and zero defect thinking was to identify and attack the waste and barriers in the administrative evaluation system in Stage One and to redesign a viable solution to allow the district to fully engage the potential of its administrators in delivering value to key stakeholders in Stage Two.

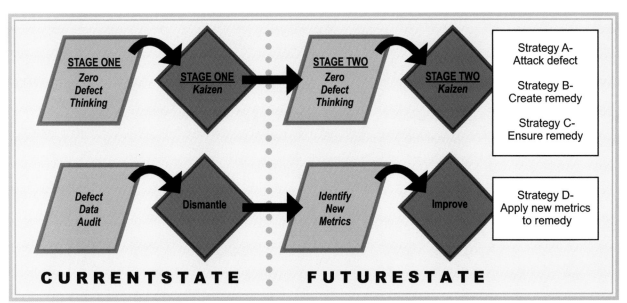

Figure 4.13- Stage One and Stage Two Kaizen and Zero Defect Thinking

For successful kaizen and zero defect thinking, the superintendent had to be willing to engage in difficult learning conversations about the administrative evaluation process, starting with "What are we doing wrong?" in Stage One and leading to "What can we do better?" in Stage Two. In this case, the kaizen event was a "blitz" of the entire process, a total dismantling and rebuilding, which directly impacted administrators, students, parents, teachers, the human resources department, and the superintendent's office.

There are many benefits of engaging in kaizen and zero defect thinking. In the end, any lean improvements for this district must positively impact mission and vision, ultimately connecting to increases in student outcomes. While the revising of the administrator evaluation process could have been handled in different ways, such as the Superintendent mandating (and then checking for compliance) of new protocols, this Lean Essentials approach was selected because it extended the designing, deploying and debriefing of the initiative to new levels of organizational capacity. The structure, standards, and deliverables of kaizen and zero defect thinking resulted in high levels of explicit stakeholder engagement and accountability in the change process, shared thinking regarding root causes and quality problem solving of viable, job-embedded solutions. Kaizen and zero defect thinking required thoughtful organization, constant support, steady commitment, and leadership from the superintendent. In all, benefits were realized to the district, the key stakeholders, the various committee members and the superintendent herself with these changes to the administrative evaluation system.

Critical Attributes of the Tool: Kaizen

- Use the tool to promote collective problem identification, analysis and solution.
- Keep kaizen focused on process improvement, not blaming people, upholding the standards of zero defect thinking.
- Move kaizen along quickly and conduct kaizen regularly, selecting the proper venue based on the scope of the project.

Critical Attributes of the Concept: Zero Defect Thinking

- Use data, not emotion, to drive thinking in Stages 1 and 2.
- Examine the current state to reconstruct it.
- Use worst case scenarios to drive improvements into the future state.

Leadership Coaching:

To begin using Kaizen and Zero Defect Thinking:

1. Identify and scope a process needing improvement.
2. Establish the kaizen venue-Blitz, Shark Attack, Daily Huddle.
3. Clarify the standards of kaizen-Do Not Create, Accept, Pass Along Defects.
4. Commit to Stage One and Stage Two Kaizen.
5. Use the Data Defect Audit to drive Stage One Kaizen and Zero Defect Thinking.
6. Use Strategies A-D to drive Stage Two Kaizen and Zero Defect Thinking.
6. Use New Metric Identification to finalize Stage Two Kaizen and Zero Defect Thinking.
7. Pilot and test solutions.
8. Keep solutions in continuous improvement and data-driven decision making.

The Concept: Leader Standard Work
The Tool: 5S

This final chapter presents a fifth Lean Essentials concept, a lean concept, leader standard work, and a lean tool, 5S. This concept and tool is useful for lean leaders interested in enhancing the management of their schools by creating clear expectations of organizational performance and high levels of employee engagement in essential protocols for work.

Since school systems are multifaceted, it is common to traditionalize ways of engaging in leadership work with equal complexity. However, it is a fallacy that leadership work must be convoluted within complex systems. For this is like adding a second scoop of ice cream to a cone designed to hold one scoop—the cone does not have the structural capacity to hold the second scoop of ice cream. In other words, if leadership work is the scoop of ice cream and the organization's degree of complexity is the cone, then adding complexity to leadership work, the second scoop of ice cream, will result in failure in the structure as the cone cannot sustain the extra complexity. When the structure of the organization gives way under the burden of byzantine leadership, the enterprise may fall apart. That second scoop of ice cream will topple off as the cone's structure crumples.

Such is the relationship of the complexity of leadership work to the fidelity of the organization. The work of leaders does not have to be multifarious within the context of organizational systems. Rather, the work of leaders should be streamlined to minimize strain and tension on the organization. This can be done by right sizing work effort, rather than expanding work effort, to diminish, rather than to enhance the thorny labyrinth of processes.

The pressure is considerable that is created by leaders when maintaining the paradigm that work complexity must extend beyond system complexity. The paradigm of adhering to overly complex leader work routines creates a metaphorical "second scoop" of confusion to taxed systems. This dynamic can put leaders in the no-win situation of working harder to meet the needs of the organization, rather than identifying and improving points of system failure. This leadership problem can be solved if it recognized as a mismatch of leadership work to the needs of the organization. The Lean Essentials, the concept of leader standard work and the 5S tool, can help leaders to accomplish the right balance between streamlining work and supporting needed complexity.

The concept of leader standard work draws on the recreation of habits of head, heart and hands through standardizing and sustaining best practice by the lean tool, 5S. In fact, the lean concept, leader standard work, and the lean tool, the 5S, can be powerful means of optimizing complex systems through the creation of work routines that streamline, rather than strain, the organization. In this chapter leader standard work and the 5S tool are described as a way to strengthen organizations.

The concept of leader standard work enacts a strategy for improving current practice by focusing on work process first and results second. Cultivating a better process of work is something that is often intended, but overlooked, in school leadership. Often an inverse relationship exists between work process and work product. As work processes become more oblique, work products become the desired benchmark of performance. This trend often causes school leaders to concentrate on work product and to avoid or to neglect work processes. And as higher positions of leadership are considered in schools, the more oblique the work processes become. Based on this rationale, the need for work process improvement actually increases within the hierarchy of the organization. The ambiguous nature of leadership can create an assumption that little or nothing can be done to create shared understandings and protocols because of these complications. However, leader standard work addresses that assumption and provides a means to eliminate confusion. The 5S tool and the concept of leader standard work can help leaders to readily improve work and to operationalize those improvements.

The 5S tool consists of five steps of work, carried out as an iterative process, that results in leader standard work. These five steps are:

1. Sorting - identifying steps, elements or activities that are critical or required to an operation or process and setting aside those that are not critical or required,
2. Setting - prioritizing and categorizing those steps, elements or activities that are critical or required to an operation or process,
3. Shining - improving the steps, elements or activities that are critical or required to an operation or process,
4. Standardizing - developing culture, climate and accountability by using the improvements in the steps, elements, or activities in the improved operation or process so that they are accepted and expected, and
5. Sustaining - creating rewards, recognitions, incentives and maintenance for keeping the improvements in steps, elements, or activities in the improved operation or process.

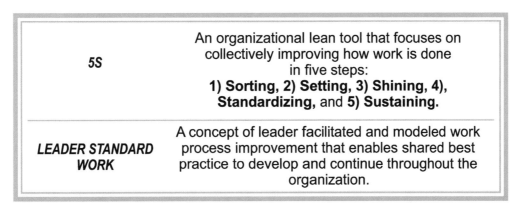

5S	An organizational lean tool that focuses on collectively improving how work is done in five steps: **1) Sorting, 2) Setting, 3) Shining, 4), Standardizing,** and **5) Sustaining.**
LEADER STANDARD WORK	A concept of leader facilitated and modeled work process improvement that enables shared best practice to develop and continue throughout the organization.

The following example illustrates how the concept of leader standard work and the 5S tool can be used by school leaders. The setting of this scene is in an elementary building at an after school meeting of the School Improvement Team (SIT) and principal. The SIT is composed of a chair and five other teachers from the building. They have been focused on data driven decision making, so the SIT is trying to examine achievement data objectively and to make decisions to improve instruction from that information. There is a high degree of trust between the SIT and the principal in this school, so the conversations in the bi-monthly SIT meetings are very honest and direct. The school is familiar with lean tools and tenets and has been learning to use them over the last year.

The principal and SIT have examined recent student achievement data in reading. The reading scores for a group of children from a particular teacher's classroom, Mr. Franc's, were not adequate. This was an unfortunate result in reading achievement for the school.

So, the SIT chair begins to talk about the data, focused on this third grade reading information, "Since we are using data to drive school improvement decisions, here we see that there are some students from Mr. Franc's third grade class with poor reading scores. It seems like the next logical step is to use this data and ask Mr. Franc to improve his reading instruction. We know that teacher quality is a major factor in student failure."

The principal looks at the SIT and states, "My opinion is that we are not gaining anything by blaming Mr. Franc for these scores. We have to understand the root cause of the reading achievement problems. So, let me restate this for clarity, we must figure out why the scores are not adequate and use our data to help us to do that. If we focus on Mr. Franc's teaching without root cause analysis, then we may add more complexity to this problem than is needed. We need to figure out what is causing this problem and then fix it. If Mr. Franc's teaching does in fact to be improved, then steps will be taken to improve his teaching. Let's pick another leading strategy as a first move."

The SIT chair is startled by this view and says, "These children are not prepared and someone is responsible. Let's keep this simple."

The principal smiles and says, "How do we know that Mr. Franc is to blame? For students to learn to read and to achieve adequate reading scores is a complex process. Have we examined this process carefully so that we can actually pinpoint Mr. Franc's teaching as the problem? What do we know about our process of teaching and assessing reading? What improvements have we made in those instructional processes? I ask this because I want to be sure that we focus on the process of teaching, not just on the work product of teaching."

The SIT thinks for a moment and they collectively respond, "This is an interesting idea to focus on process improvement, not just on results. We do look at our data and we conduct line item test analyses to make small adjustments in the instructional process, but we do not have a shared understanding of the total instructional process yet."

The principal continues, "That is what I am thinking, also. We do know that teacher quality is the most impactful element, but we must look at the students' learning experience as a system to properly fix this problem. Elements such as the student's prior knowledge of reading, the level of reading skill development, the quality of previous instruction, the nature and design of our assessments, the degree of parental involvement in promoting reading, the levels of environmental stress--as well as quality of the teaching all contribute to success and failure."

"Yes, but that is hard to figure out," replies the SIT chair, "How can we handle this so as to be able to better understand the process of reading instruction?"

The principal explains, "If we choose to blame one teacher for student achievement gaps without a good root cause analysis, then we will never improve reading instruction. A focus on work product must be intertwined with process improvement. In fact, acting before root cause analysis could create additional confusing dynamics that will pit teachers against each other and hurt our students. We need to strengthen the reading instructional system first by examining root causes of failure, categorizing and prioritizing those root causes of failure, and then by improving, standardizing and sustaining best instructional practice. Certainly, if Mr. Franc proves to be an incompetent teacher of reading after 5S process improvement, then appropriate administrative action will be taken. Let's keep our approach simple by not blaming people as a leading strategy. Instead, I suggest that we collectively engage in 5S work so that leader standard work can develop for reading instruction. I encourage us to focus on improving processes based on eliminating the root causes of failure and developing standardized reading instructional practices in a way that will make a difference to our students' achievement."

The SIT members nod in agreement, "OK, that is reasonable. We do not want to cause additional problems. We want to improve our school."

The principal in this elementary school introduced the concept of leader standard work and the use of the tool, 5S, to the SIT in order to keep them from wasting time and energy by adding complexity to reading instruction. The reason for this approach is because leader standard work will keep the school focused on improving reading instruction by managing the system of instruction better through 5S analysis. It is a natural tendency to focus the blame for problems on something or someone. In this case, the blame was pointed to one person, Mr. Franc, for the reading achievement failures. However, acting in this manner by blaming Mr. Franc without systemic analysis, although it seemed very straightforward to the SIT at first, would consequently cause a repertoire of problems. Furthermore, if Mr. Franc was not, in fact, the key problem in reading instruction in the building, by blaming Mr. Franc initially, the SIT runs the risk that they are leaving reading instruction shortfalls in place in the school. Blaming Mr. Franc absent leader standard work and 5S analysis could result in negative implications, including dividing the school, confusing the instructional culture, or inducing additional school improvement and administrator work.

The principal was trying to avoid a common pattern of ignoring work process improvement. He worried that the end result of not using leader standard work and the 5S tool would be to add more complexity to instructional work within the context of a multi-faceted instructional system. Concerned that the SIT and the principal might have to divert their focus on school improvement work to keeping the faculty united in dealing with Mr. Franc's repercussions, for instance, would be a setback for the school. Overall, the original suggestion to target Mr. Franc as a leading strategy to reduce the shortfall in reading scores would inevitably take away from a core focus on instructional improvement. Blaming Mr. Franc would be like adding a second scoop of complexity to the delicate cone of reading instruction.

The principal instead wanted to steer the school improvement team into the use of the Lean Essentials, leader standard work and the 5S tool. This approach has the potential to create better instructional alignment and more clarity so that reading instruction is delivered better. To move forward on this strategy, leader standard work and the 5S tool begin with "cleaning house," so to speak, by moving through five steps. The first step is getting rid of teaching methods and paradigms that are not effective. The second step is sorting through the complexities of the learning environment so that top tier problems are recognized. The third step is further targeting and mastering what matters to student achievement. The fourth step is standardizing aspects of reading instruction so as to reduce waste in retaining, searching and waiting for solutions to develop. The fifth step is sustaining those improvements.

Back in the meeting room with the SIT, the principal moves to the whiteboard and asks the diligent committee to list all of the elements in the instructional environment in the process of third grade reading that matter to the at risk student reader. Six ideas were placed on the board, including, 1) utilization of a good reading curriculum, 2) reading assessment and intervention, 3) appropriate instructional technology, 4) authentic reading pedagogy, 5) formative testing strategies, and 6) high levels of faculty and parental teamwork.

"Is this the list of six key elements for good reading achievement for our at risk students?" asks the principal.

"We should add one more," one committee member speaks up. "What about the degree of differentiation and personalization afforded these students?"

"OK, great, let's add that one," the principal adds this seventh element, degree of differentiation and personalization, to the board. "Is there anything else?"

"Yes," says another member, "we should add something about relationships, the need for learning to be interpersonal, social and emotional. Also, don't forget the quality of the reading instruction, the quality of the teacher."

"Good!" said the principal and the last two items were added to the list on the board. Since the SIT members had finished the list of nine items, the principal instructed, "Now, let's look at our students who failed reading and walk in their shoes, so that we can sort out what does matter to them. This is the first step of the 5S tool, Sorting. Let's look at this list that we need to sort through." The SIT read through the list:

5S: Sorting Out What Matters in Reading Instruction to At Risk Students

1. Utilizing a good reading curriculum
2. Timely assessment and intervention
3. Appropriate instructional technology
4. Shared authentic pedagogy
5. Formative testing strategies

6. Faculty and parental team work
7. Degree of differentiation and personalization
8. Amount of interpersonal, social and emotional learning
9. Quality of reading instruction

The principal describes the next task. "As a school improvement team, I would like you to compare each of these nine items by creating a current state value stream map of our first through third grade student readers who are at risk. These students are the customers on the value stream map, so we will work to understand what is most valuable to them. Use these nine elements you have identified here as metrics of importance for reading success." The SIT agrees to create nine value stream maps, with each map focusing on each of the nine elements. They divide up this task and decide to complete their work in two weeks in time for the next meeting.

When the SIT meets again in two weeks, there was a value stream for each of the nine items. Each map is examined and kaizen bursts are added where improvements are needed, creating the basis for the future state map. Interestingly, the value stream map for Item #2, "Timely reading assessment and intervention," has the most kaizen bursts. The committee decides that this element of reading instruction is a top priority process in dire need of improvement.

The principal is pleased that a deeper understanding of the work processes of reading instruction is developing as these nine items are sorted into two priority improvement piles, "Needs Immediate Improvement" and "Needs Improvement," and one discard pile, "Does Not Need Improvement." Item #2 ended up in the "Needs Immediate Improvement" category, Items #4, #6, #7, #8, and #9 ended up in the "Needs Improvement" category, and Items #1, #3, and #5 ended up in the "Does Not Need Improvement" category. Leader standard work is becoming clearer as the first two steps of the 5S tool are used by the SIT, Sorting and Setting.

The Sorting step enables the SIT to figure out which elements were on the original list and further, which of the nine elements should remain on the table for improvement and which ones could be set aside. As the current state value stream maps were studied and kaizen was used, it became obvious that three of the items, #1, #3, and #5, in their current states were very strong. These three items were placed into the "Does Not Need Improvement" category. Sorting is the first step of 5S work because it creates one "red tag" or discard pile that can be set aside. In this case, the SIT understands that three of the nine elements were qualified to be "red tagged" and set aside because they did not need improvement.

The Setting step further helps the SIT to understand which of the remaining six elements were most problematic or constraining to the delivery of reading instruction. The current state value stream maps and kaizen work highlight how dysfunctional Item #2, "Timely reading assessment and intervention," was compared to the other five elements. The Setting step leads the SIT to create two more categories of work, "Needs Immediate Improvement," for Item #2, and "Needs Improvement," for Items #4, #6, #7, #8, and #9. The SIT writes down the results of Sorting and Setting on the board as:

5S: Sorting and Setting Reading Instruction Improvement Work

SORTING	Item
Red Tag / Discard *"Does Not Need Improvement"*	1. Utilizing a good reading curriculum 3. Appropriate instructional technology 5. Formative testing strategies

SETTING	Item
High Priority *"Needs Immediate Improvement"*	2. Timely assessment and intervention

MODERATE PRIORITY	Item
High Priority *"Needs Improvement"*	4. Shared authentic pedagogy 6. Faculty and parental team work 7. Degree of differentiation and personalization 8. Amount of interpersonal, social and emotional learning 9. Quality of reading instruction

The current state value stream map for Item #2, "Timely assessment and intervention," represents the Response-to-Intervention (RtI) program in this school for reading instruction. The RtI program is highly regarded by the school and is required by mandate, so the SIT wants to make sure the school was implementing RtI well. What the kaizen bursts of the current state value stream map reveals were that there were major problems in identifying students in a timely fashion as pre-qualified for potential reading intervention.

The current state value stream map and kaizen for RtI in the school depicts a lengthy process for presenting students for testing by pre-qualifying the students based on learning problems. To pre-qualify a student with a learning problem, formative methods of two cycles of assessment were used where the at risk student was tested every marking period to judge the status of the student's reading. This student would read to a teacher every ten weeks. The teacher would document the reading. After two cycles, or twenty weeks, it was determined if the student pre-qualified for possible RtI services.

The current state value stream map showed that the metrics for timely reading assessment and intervention were way off because the process took too long to create value for the at risk student. The pre-qualifying process covered a minimum of twenty weeks, or two cycles of testing, and after that time, it still had to be determined if the student apparently needing assistance might qualify for it. The written documentation process of two ten-week progress monitoring cycles was very complete, but it left the floundering student struggling for half a school year without assistance.

The SIT was able to pinpoint the waste in this process through the current state value stream map using the Metric of Timely Intervention. Further, they were able to make concrete recommendations for school improvement that could be carried out right away and piloted for the next few weeks. The committee decided that the progress monitoring would be reduced to five weeks and that student work samples could also be provided as formatively-based documentation of a need. The allocation of time required for the ten week progress monitoring would remain the same, but it would be consolidated to a five week timeline with the addition of the student work samples. This change saved fifteen weeks in the pre-qualifying cycle.

As the SIT finalizes their thoughts about this recommendation, the principal comments, "What you have accomplished in two weeks is that you have started to create leader standard work. You have created an improvement in the RtI pre-qualifying process in two weeks, by finishing the first two steps of the 5S tool, Sorting, Setting, and starting a piloting period for Shining the recommended cycle reduction. The 5S lean tool will also help you to complete the Shine step and to eventually

93

Standardize and Sustain best practice around timely reading assessment and intervention as the school moves forward."

The SIT was able to complete the first two steps of the 5S, Sorting and Setting, and to begin the third step of Shining rather quickly within the context of these two meetings because they used value stream mapping and kaizen as visual management tools. This helped the SIT to move through Sorting, Setting and to start Shining.

Since the 5S process of Sorting, Setting, Shining, Standardizing, and Sustaining improvement is well underway, the principal explains, "You have completed the first three steps of the 5S, by Sorting, Setting, and Shining. So, let's review what you have accomplished in terms of leader standard work. When you first listed out the key elements of reading instruction, the first 'S,' Sorting, you created the list of nine elements. When you created and examined current value stream maps, you completed a quick kaizen for each of them, you were able to figure out that three elements did not need your attention. These three items were "Red Tagged" and set aside. Sorting, therefore, helped you to distinguish where to focus your energy and where not to focus your energy. Also, as you examined the kaizen bursts, you were able to prioritize which of the remaining six processes were most problematic. Using the second 'S,' Setting, these six elements were placed into two categories "Needs Immediate Improvement," and "Needs Improvement." Setting brought forth the importance of focusing on Item #2, the reading assessment and intervention element. Since you selected this as a pressing need to immediately improve, this most problematic element of the timeliness of reading assessment and intervention and did complete a kaizen for it, you have started the third 'S,' Shining. The third 'S,' Shining, began when you introduced improvements to the RtI student qualification process as a pilot and created a future state value stream map based on your kaizen. So, the changed timeline and the addition of student work samples mean that reading assessment and intervention will be better tomorrow that it was today for our school. We will complete Shining as the suggested improvement is piloted further in the next five weeks, data is collected, and the improvement is finalized."

The principal adds this information to the SIT chart created earlier in this meeting on the board as:

94

5S: Sorting, Setting and Shining Reading Instruction Improvement Work	
SORTING	**Item**
Red Tag / Discard	
"Does Not Need Improvement"	1. Utilizing a good reading curriculum
	3. Appropriate instructional technology
	5. Formative testing strategies
SETTING	**Item**
High Priority	
"Needs Immediate Improvement"	2. Timely assessment and intervention
MODERATE PRIORITY	**Item**
High Priority	
"Needs Improvement"	4. Shared authentic pedagogy
	6. Faculty and parental team work
	7. Degree of differentiation and personalization
	8. Amount of interpersonal, social and emotional learning
	9. Quality of reading instruction
SHINING	**Item**
High Priority	
"Needs Improvement"	2. Timely assessment and intervention
Improvement: Minimize pre-qualifying time of RTI process from twenty weeks to five weeks by allowing student work as the formative assessment process.	
Implement: Pilot these improvements for the next five weeks.	

As the SIT examines the progress made, the SIT chair speaks up, "So, how do we finish the 5S process and get to leader standard work?"

The principal replies, "To finish the 5S process and to get to leader standard work, you will have to be sure that your suggested improvements actually work. This will be determined by data we collect in the pilot. So, let's say that we collect three sets of data over the next five weeks. How reasonable would it be for us to collect data on: 1) at risk student time to pre-qualification for intervention, 2) if pre-qualified, the quality of remaining RtI roll out, and 3) improvements in student reading?"

An SIT member speaks up, "The first data set is fairly easy to collect, but we will not catch all at risk students on the second metric. The third data set can also be tracked."

"OK," the principal pauses, "So, are these data sets are helpful to us in terms of understanding if the new, reduced process of timely assessment and intervention creates value for our at risk student readers?"

Another SIT member nods, "Since this 5S step is a Shine, we will either be able to collect and use the data to see if the change works or we will find out that the data sets don't inform us adequately and we can go back and collect different data." There is consensus from the SIT on this suggestion.

The principal concludes, "As we complete the Shining step, we will want to be very confident in this improvement because the next step is Standardizing. We do not want to Standardize our reading instruction around a poor process. That is what we are trying to change! So, here is what we have so far on our 5S work. Does this represent what we have discussed?" Everyone reviews what is on the board as:

5S: Sorting, Setting and Shining Reading Instruction Improvement Work	
SORTING	**Item**
Red Tag / Discard	
"Does Not Need Improvement"	1. Utilizing a good reading curriculum
	3. Appropriate instructional technology
	5. Formative testing strategies
SETTING	**Item**
High Priority	
"Needs Immediate Improvement"	2. Timely assessment and intervention
MODERATE PRIORITY	**Item**
High Priority	
"Needs Improvement"	4. Shared authentic pedagogy
	6. Faculty and parental team work
	7. Degree of differentiation and personalization
	8. Amount of interpersonal, social and emotional learning
	9. Quality of reading instruction
SHINING	**Item**
High Priority	
"Needs Improvement"	2. Timely assessment and intervention

Improvement: Minimize pre-qualifying time of RTI process from twenty weeks to five weeks by allowing student work as the formative assessment process.
Implement: Pilot these improvements for the next five weeks.
Document changes in:
1) at risk student time to intervention,
2) quality of intervention rolled out, and
3) improvements in student reading.

The SIT chair concurs, *"This looks good. Can you give us some guidance on the last two 5S steps?"*

The principal continues, "The fourth 'S,' Standardizing, will help us to get used to and to routinize the final Shining improvements. Since we are careful in Shining, the third 'S,' to avoid standardizing around poor solutions, the changes are not mandated. However, after we pilot them and set up ways to capture three data sets as measures of improved performance, we can ascertain if the shined assessment and intervention process works well. So, over the next five weeks, let's try this new method, check the data and then we will be ready to move from Shining to Standardizing. During the next five weeks of Shining, I would like this improvement to be discussed at our weekly faculty meetings at least twice."

A SIT member interrupts, "OK, so we have five weeks to complete the third 'S,' Shining, and then we will be ready to move into the fourth 'S,' Standardizing. This means that we will be mandating this change at the Standardizing step, right?"

The principal nods, "That is correct, almost. If we find we have problems with the proposed changes with the Standardizing step, then we do not want to standardize. But, if we find that the changes improve our process of reading instruction of our students, then we will Standardize. This step should include training the faculty and establishing cultural expectations for transitioning through the change."

The SIT chair asks, "So, then what is the last 'S?' Once we have this solution standardized, what is next?"

The principal says, "Once we know that we have the best possible solution in place, we have to be sure that everyone understands it and can do it. That will wrap up Standardizing. Then, we are ready to Sustain it, the fifth 'S.' In Sustaining this improvement, I will be responsible for making sure the improvement is maintained over time. In the end, as you and I have created leader standard work through the 5S, my job is to create leader standard work around Sustaining this improvement. So, I will have to change the way that I lead this building in that I will make sure that the improved process remains in place. The small amount of time that it will take me to make sure that this improvement is Sustained is easier than allowing the new practice to slip away and for the old problems to surface again. Are there any questions?"

The SIT meeting was readied for dismissal, so the SIT chair was assigned the task of informing the faculty of the pilot and fielding a discussion at two subsequent faculty meetings. The other SIT members volunteered to collect the three data sets and post the results on a weekly basis on the data wall in the lunchroom.

The principal identifies a lunch time in three days that would serve as a brown bag session for teachers to ask questions and receive further information. These activities complete the Shine work.

The principal also makes a commitment to reconvene with the SIT after the five week pilot was complete to determine if the change would be Standardized. As a part of the Standardization, the principal also indicates that the faculty would be trained, as needed. Once through the four 5S steps, the principal states that he will then Sustain the improvement, completing the 5S cycle through leader standard work.

The school relies on the visual management work of the SIT data collectors throughout the five week pilot to track the work and post the weekly results in order to help the school understand what was taking place. Along with the faculty meeting discussions and a brown bag lunch, the whole school became aware of this improvement under consideration.

After the pilot was completed, the SIT examines the data and finds that the improvement worked well in moving students through the pre-qualifying stage in a timely manner. This completed the Shine step and led to the Standardize step.

The faculty were formally trained in the changed process and given two weeks to get used to it in the Sustain step. The principal and SIT fields faculty questions following a hands-on orientation session at the weekly faculty meeting.

This set up the school for the final step in 5S, Sustaining. The principal is now responsible for completing the 5S cycle by using leader standard work to keep the improvement in place. The principal ooks closely over the remainder of the year for positive answers to questions, such as, "Is there a clear understanding of what this improvement is in the pre-qualification of students for RTI?", "Is the improvement now standard practice in reading instruction?" and "Is third grade reading achievement improving or is there another shortfall that we need to attack?" The completion of 5S did create leader standard work for the Principal, work understood by the SIT and the faculty.

Over a seven-week time period, the use of the 5S tool and the leader standard work concept cleared up a key barrier to student reading achievement. As the SIT continues to maintain the data wall; it is easy for entire building to track reading achievement this way. There is also a place on the data wall for teacher suggestions to be posted and they are reviewed and discussed at the faculty meetings.

As progress is celebrated, the SIT continues its work on improving reading instruction, starting with the next category of problems, "Needs Improvement." The SIT asks the principal to continue to facilitate 5S to create leader standard work based on next element selected as before. Based on the examination of the current state value stream maps and the kaizen bursts, the next improvement strategy is selected. As time progressed, the principal makes Sustaining his leader standard work and the SIT made Sorting, Setting, Shining, and Standardizing the precursor to leader standard work.

The benefits of 5S and leader standard work are that school improvement activities are triggered that focus on fixing problems, rather than on blaming people. The school gained some rhythm or flow around the process of school improvement as the SIT committee works on each item, piloting improvements, maintaining a data wall, discussing what worked and what did not work. The level of communication increases greatly around reading instruction in the building. As the committee and the principal carries out leader standard work, fewer instructional mistakes are made by the school overall and shared standards of reading instruction developes. The SIT maintains a commitment to use data to drive school improvement decisions and now they have a sequence of successful strategies and tenets to use to enact this commitment. They are able to skillfully sort out where improvement is needed exactly in order to achieve reading goals. In some cases, the use of the 5S tool and leader standard work results in differentiated solutions. In other cases, common solutions are developed.

The point of this Lean Essentials tool and concept combination, 5S and leader standard work, is that it sets up the dynamics for tested change that is subject to several feedback and improvement loops before it gets rolled out. It gives organizations a chance to build some intelligence around an idea and to identify best practice. When supplemented with visual management tools, such as the value stream map or data walls; working documents, such as 5S reports; and regular assignments aligned with the changes, the potential for improvement success is very high.

Schools may be weighed down by many different types of problems that could benefit greatly from the 5S tool and leader standard work. For example, a dress code for a school may appear to be a very straightforward process to carry out, but often there are many factors that surround dress code management that create variations and confusion. If a student wears a 'hoodie" to class and is spotted coming from a teacher's room with the hood up, it is easy to find blame. For instance, it is possible to blame the teacher for not enforcing the policy, to blame the administration for not enforcing the policy, to blame the parent for allowing the student to wear the hoodie, and to blame the student for not following the dress code policy. When this blaming routine becomes standard practice and takes root in a school, the process of dress code management becomes very complex. In some cases, it becomes so obtuse that teachers and administrators just give up and ignore the policy. This is not to suggest that each of these stakeholders, the teacher, the administrator, the parent or the student should not be held accountable for not following or enforcing the school policy. But, rather, that before placing blame, the leading strategy should focus on whether the policy and policy enforcement is a mess and needs to be put into a 5S analysis, beginning with Sorting and followed by Setting and the remaining three 'S' steps, Shining, Standardizing and Sustaining.

If the dress code policy is not being managed well, for example, the 5S process can help a principal, administrative team or teacher leader team to figure out what the core problem is (Setting and Sorting), to bring forth changes and to test those changes for fidelity in getting rid of or minimizing the problem (Sorting and Shining), and last, to create and maintain routines, traditions and protocols around new best practice (Standardizing and Sustaining).

There are many uses of the Lean Essentials, the 5S and leader standard work. The 5S creates the opportunity for leader standard work to get established so that positive culture develops around continuous improvement. In this way, best practice can be maintained, rather than lost, with reworking the same problems minimized.

Critical Attributes of the Tool: 5S

- Use the tool to create data-driven best practice with both hard and soft processes.
- Complete the five steps, Sort, Set, Shine, Standardize, and Sustain, to ensure fidelity.
- Use visual management balanced with professional efficacy to drive success.
- Develop 5S solutions collaboratively and celebrate shared best practice.

Critical Attributes of the Concept: Leader Standard Work

- Use the concept to create and maintain continuous improvement routines.
- Set culture around clear expectations for paradigms and actions of work once shared best practice is established via 5S.
- Focus on behaviors and process improvement, not blaming.
- Avoid policing people: go for coaching, teaching and peer review to sustain gains.

Leadership Coaching:

To begin using 5S and Leader Standard Work:

1. Collectively identify a core barrier and focus on developing best practice for solution longevity.
2. Stage the five steps of 5S and begin to focus on leader standard work as the process unfolds.
3. Engage in leader standard work as a way to develop organizational authenticity.
4. Minimize the complexity of work as a way of improving and sustaining complex processes

PROLOGUE

This book has presented school leaders with five different Lean Essentials, paired lean concepts and tools, used in a variety of scenarios. To summarize, the Lean Essentials and scenarios are:

Chapter One
> Lean Essentials -
> The Concept: Overproduction
> The Tool: The Five Why's
> The Scenario: Improving a Teacher Advisor Program, Part I, Through Root Cause Analysis

Chapter Two
> Lean Essentials -
> The Concept: Learning to See Waste
> The Tool: Value Stream Mapping
> The Scenario: Improving a Teacher Advisor Program, Part II, Through Stakeholder Metrics

Chapter Three
> Lean Essentials -
> The Concept: Plan-Do-Check-Adjust Thinking
> The Tool: A3
> The Scenario: Improving Special Education Delivery Through Process Improvement

Chapter Four
> Lean Essentials -
> The Concept: Zero Defect Thinking
> The Tool: Kaizen
> The Scenario: Improving Administrative Evaluation Through Elimination of Process Defects

Chapter Five
> Lean Essentials -
> The Concept: Leader Standard Work
> The Tool: 5S
> The Scenario: Improving Reading Instruction Through Sustaining Best Practice

Through a broad stroke, this book introduces school leaders to basic lean concepts and tools. A variety of scenarios common to many in school leadership are examined. The book demonstrates how these lean concepts and tools can be used as independent Lean Essentials as concept/tool pairs. And to a limited degree, it also depicts how these lean concepts and tools can be used as one interdependent Lean Essentials System. The book is not intended as a prescription, but as a guideline as to how enact lean thinking and applications successfully in schools. The descriptions, anecdotes and analyses are presented to assist school leaders with viewing typical problems through the lens of lean improvement. Each scenario is based on realistic and relevant problems faced by school leaders.

For interested educators, the challenges of lean concepts and tools do require a commitment to a learning journey. It takes some time to grasp the significance of applying lean to leadership practice. The book offers educators the opportunity to comprehend and assimilate how this bevy of individual or combined Lean Essentials may better equip them to serve schools with more savvy, acumen and confidence in the future.

After reading this book, one may wonder how to begin to engage as a student of lean. My best advice is to select one Lean Essential, one tool and one concept pair, and to use it on a small scale immediately. For instance, in the next meeting you attend, invariably a problem will be present. In this case, you could use the Lean Essentials, the lean tool, the Five Why's to figure out what the root cause of the problem is, and then use the concept of Overproduction to ascertain where waste is occurring in the processes surrounding the problem.

If you will step out and begin to apply your Lean Essentials, lean concepts and lean tools in small ways, you will likely begin to understand the benefits of doing so. Each new time that lean tools and concepts are used, lean practitioners attest that processes become cleaner, more focused, and more productive; results become better, more systemic, and more impactful; and people become collaborative, more sophisticated, and more driven by improvement. As you progress in your lean journey, you will find ways to understand and apply individual Lean Essentials as a Lean Essentials System. In other words, if you begin to use lean, the benefits of using lean and will begin to surface for you. And you will become more sophisticated in your application of lean as well.

In closing, for school leaders who have used individual Lean Essentials or Lean Essential Systems, they report one additional benefit—excitement! Lean is fun to use as it improves both how work gets done and what work results in. It is hoped that as lean is used more in schools, that the contributions of masterful educational leaders will create educational potential beyond the limits of what is commonly accepted practice. Enjoy the journey!

CPSIA information can be obtained at www.ICGtesting.com
Printed in the USA
LVIW01n0855090417
530154LV00008B/47